THE POWER
OF
PERSONAL PRESENCE

Jane Hundley

Image Training Center
16301 NE 8th
Suite 230,
Bellevue, Washington 98008
206-957-1996

CenterPoint Publishing
Bellevue, Washington

Dedication

This book is dedicated to my parents,
James R. Hundley, D.V.M. and Charlotte D. Hundley
with gratitude, love and respect.
And to
my grandmother,
Mrs. Philip Delano
for giving me the best memories a child could ever have.

Acknowledgements

Witness, for revealing to me the message of this book.

David Hutton, my husband, partner and friend for his constant support, recommendations and encouragement and for teaching me the value of patience.

Delphine and Estelle Heron, my daughters, for being born such incredible individuals who have positively shaped my life and for giving me quiet time to write.

Homer and Wilmaglen Bergren, for their endorsement and genuine interest in my work throughout the years.

Sheryn Hara, for her promotional talents and urging me to complete this book.

Allen Auvil, for his generosity in time and creative energy on the illustrations and cover design.

Tim Asher for final cover design.

Fredric Lehrman, for photographing the cover picture and supporting me.

Louise Peyrot, for always assisting me at the right time.

Sharon Henning, for her sincere friendship in life that empowers me to see my strengths.

All my clients and workshop participants, for wanting to discover and express their true power and presence.

"All islands meet beneath the sea."

Unknown

Table Of Contents

Introduction

*"I have lived on the lip
of insanity, wanting to know reasons,
knocking on a door. It opens.
I've been knocking from the inside!"*
Rumi

We live in a world of form and image. Image can be compared, shaped, changed, manipulated, judged and redesigned. Though a pleasing image is an asset that can improve the quality of our lives, it cannot give us more worth—and a sense of worth is what we seek. We will not find that worth in any external pursuit of image transformation, because we are more than what we appear to be. We are an inner essence that resides within a form and which has an image. Our essence is genuinely worthy. As an inner essence of truth, we cannot be increased or decreased, compared, judged, shaped, or changed, except in perception.

A wave of heated discontent is growing among consumers about the perception that image denotes worth. It is time to change the perception. Each of us, regardless of our external form and image is equally worthy, but we do not equally feel that worth. Not one advertising company, business or fashion mogul has the power to change our internal perception of ourselves. That is our job alone. The more we search externally to find our worth, or dig externally to find blame, the more disappointed and frustrated we will be. It is imperative to turn within and find truth, a truth that is not dependent on external forms. When we do this, our perceptions and myths about image will change from a disempowering one to an empowerment process, because truth allows us to know our worth, true power and unique purpose. Truth is always healing, empowering and transforming.

My research in the past twenty years working within the image industry has been divided between two seemingly opposing directions—internal and external. Contrary to how life appears to be, the world of reality is internal, and the world of illusion is external. Though I have spent half of my life nestled in the world of illusory image as a *projection* of self, my personal focus has been directed toward the internal reality of *true expression* of self. I have followed a compelling path of discovering how these two worlds come together—in our own bodies, in our own experience of life.

As a world traveler observing people from many other cultures, I have found that all people have the same desire: Fulfillment. What makes them individually different are their definitions of fulfillment and methods of striving towards it. Many people have not defined fulfillment nor chosen any methods to achieve it. This lack of direction creates a feeling of being lost—even helpless—about their future.

We all have an innate yearning to *belong*. We want to be able to be ourselves and have others around us recognize our fundamental human worth. We want to reach our human potential. This is a longing that runs deep in the consciousness of every man, woman and child. To be recognized is a basic birthright that is linked to self-fulfillment.

Fulfillment is an intricately woven spiral of our inner worth and outer assets. Achieving goals, dreams and desires in pleasing external forms is a creative focus of building assets. Discovering the true self within, claiming authentic power and expressing life purpose is to accept internal worth.

One without the other seems lacking somehow. But if we could only choose one, then knowing inherent worth is more rewarding because a sense of worth is an achievement that endures the tests of time. Our worth is constant, but our assets are changing and not permanent.

However, many people pursue personal growth to increase their outer assets, which is a noble endeavor in its own right. They want more assets, such as money, friends, material comforts, timE, intimacy and vacations. They want to have better communication as managers, parents and partners. They want to have a better body image, better jobs and better relationships.

They also want what money, friends, material comforts, time, intimacy and vacations *represent* to them, which is more freedom, safety, love, understanding and well-being. They want to empower their children, reduce conflict and stress and have a better rapport with their bosses and co-workers. They want to communicate clearly and be understood. They want to understand their behavior, change unwanted and unconscious habits and enjoy their lives. They want self-esteem.

They seek fulfillment which, intrinsically, is an internal experience independent of the outer.

Isn't it honorable, though, to have both?

This pursuit of understanding inner and outer fulfillment has been the undeniable focus of my life for over twenty years.

As a student of life I am in constant awe. I have learned that we can fulfill our lives by changing the way that we respond to the world. We cannot change or control all external events, but we can empower how we respond to them, and that is the key that makes all the difference. To do this requires understanding the mind, and having the willingness to change our habits of thinking. These habits are patterns that encompass beliefs, insights, opinions and judgements. Together they form paradigms or filters that create our reality— internal AND external.

Thoughts and all that they mean to us, literally, create reality.

This is not a new idea. Ralph Waldo Emerson said, "The ancestor of every action is a thought." This was not original with him either. The truth of expanding consciousness as the key to human potential has been explored as a science for thousands of years.

What IS new is the moment when you understand that. What is continually new is your experience of it. Every time. Forever. The experience of shifting thought paradigms gets more exciting, exhilarating, rejuvenating, pleasurable and fun each time you do it. Each time you have the ability to respond and participate more fully. You experience your vitality physically, psychologically, emotionally, spiritually, and *all at the same time*. You are PRESENT, in the here and now, the only place and time where you are fully self-empowered and are able to *shift*.

In the world of form and permanent change, conscious shifting is the difference between an imbalanced life experience, and the balance of internal/external harmony.

When we do not choose a method, then life will gladly accommodate us and send us change, whether we want it or not. We have all experienced an event that had such a powerful impact that it changed the way we thought and behaved instantly. It may have been a good or bad experience, but the fact that we were fully *present* made it bond in memory. Being present is the very essence and crucial component to effective learning. Learning must take place in the now. To accomplish this we must unravel negative memories of the past through which we view the present.

Memories act either as building blocks or stumbling blocks. That depends on how you perceive the experience—positively or negatively. The ultimate key is your free will in choosing how you perceive the external world. If the memory is negative, the perception will be negative, and the results will be less than positive. If the memory is positive, then the perception and results will be positive. Creating an empowering memory is a very important process in self-fulfillment. Staying in your true power and presence is how to strengthen it.

Many people have attained phenomenal external assets and goals yet do not feel fulfilled because they do not internalize the achievement. They deflect. I was a master at deflecting my outer achievements. My external recognition as a child, teen, model and image consultant did not reward me with a true sense of my inner worth. Appearing on covers of international magazines, in editorial spreads, and working with top designers worldwide did little to foster my self-image. I had to find another way.

Life to me is a constant practice of awareness which unfolds, shapes and expresses who I really am. Everyday I am mindful of the concepts and practices illustrated in this book. I am a life-long learner who is teaching others like me, and I know that there are millions of them. Lack of self-love is the internal epidemic that permeates all our external challenges today.

My personal vision is to strengthen the positive presence and true self-love of individuals by establishing an unbreakable link between the inner and outer image. With sincerity, I invite you to discover what I have learned. Most of all, I hope that you learn to access your true self and authentic power, and to more fully express the *power of your own personal presence* in every arena of your life.

CHAPTER 1

The Heart of Image

*"I take the path that ecstatic human beings have taken for
centuries."*

Mirabai

There is a very real human desire to "co-create"
the image of the body. Image is what you *appear* to be.
It is an influential form of communication that can be
the cause of instant approval, bonding, and attraction,
or the root of misconceptions, misunderstandings and
prejudice. Improving image is a facet of personal
growth and the relentless pursuit of many people,
resulting in a multi-billion dollar body-image-fashion-
beauty industry that caters to every *imaginary* want and
need. Image is constantly changing, and the challenge
is to design it to empower you and your goals as much
as possible. Image can be managed as an asset that
creates choices, not obstacles for you.

Nevertheless, image is limited to the external
self. Though it is tangible and visible, image is still an

enigma to most of us. We strive constantly to come to terms with our image, our bodies, our selves. A plethora of television talk shows daily demonstrates the quandary we feel about image. We are trying to understand what image is really about, what our image is communicating to others, and how it personifies us. We seek to know how and when we fall short of expressing our true selves, and why. We want to know why it makes a difference to look one way or another. We are confused about who we really are, and we feel that, somehow, answering the image question will give us the key to ending that confusion. This obsession with image exists because we have a sense that *there is something much greater happening that involves image and we all intuitively know it.*

But, what is it? Answering this question is the purpose of this book. To do that, we have to go to the heart of the issue.

I first entered the image industry twenty years ago. I have spent much of my time exploring the cause and effects of external appearances. While executing hundreds of counseling sessions and consultations on image and self-image, I learned that image transformation is a process, not an event. It cannot be accomplished by simply manipulating your body language, how you shake someone's hand, walk into a room or coordinate your wardrobe. These are valuable components of a positive self-image, but they are not the keys to long-lasting positive presentation. You have to journey to the very source of yourself, go to the heart of your image by discovering who you really are. You have to look at the whole picture: *The inner and the outer you at the same time.*

There you will uncover the undeniable, intangible, but *visible* link between internal and external image.

Presence is that link. Presence is the principle that bridges your internal state and your external appearance.

Image is a visual facade, but *presence* is a synergy of expressions—an inner and outer connection of feeling, thinking and behaving effectively and with qualities that are expressed in appearance—all united at the same time, yielding a whole that is greater than the sum of its parts. Outer image is that part of the picture that makes an initial impact, but it is not the *source* or synergy of personal presence.

Personal presence is what we are really seeking—beyond image. Fashion models, television newscasters, executives, sales managers, politicians, teachers, ministers and leaders of all kinds learn effective personal *presence.* Knowing how to move through life with grace and influence are natural qualities which a person who has presence exudes. It is a complete and unique combination of the inner and outer person. Their image is only one facet of the *whole* picture of presence.

Presence is at the heart of looking your best. It honors the process of your life, the real inner you as well as the outer expression. With presence you express positive growth, credibility and true power. Without it you express negative attitudes, poor self-image and false power. When you project the power of your personal presence you convey a state of integrity, positive intention, and balance in your life. You are self-empowered, which in turn naturally empowers others around you in your family, your work and your social environment.

Descriptions of who you are become more positive and sharply defined when you are present, because you are exuding credibility. You have a stately bearing. This effect is projected through your most potent communicator of all—namely nonverbal signs and sounds which are made up of appearance, body language, and tone of voice. These outer expressions are linked to a powerful, hidden source.

Personal presence is not a form of self-manipulation, pretense or tricks to coerce others. It is not a way to learn how to vie for position, conform to others with motives for getting their approval or look good in the eyes of your superiors.

With personal presence at work you naturally become more self-possessed, assured and persuasive. You more easily strengthen your position, maintain a stable, winning strategy, and look exceptionally well to others. You gain high visibility. You bear confidence in your self-presentation because you truly are in a state of balance. You are able to achieve results in your goals, dreams and desires, and *enjoy the process* at the same time. You understand the meaning of true power and you do not play roles either socially, professionally or personally that do not empower your clear vision and purpose.

When our state of presence is disconnected we give away our true power. This happens when we don't speak up, let our bodies go to pot, think negatively, appear helpless, choose to look unattractive and disorderly, sound sarcastic, procrastinate about making necessary changes, maintain unwanted habits, feel depressed, look for approval, lack style, act with guilt and expect the worst.

All states in which we are not empowering our *presence* results in a poor communication of who we really are. We are perceived in ways that are not consistent with our potential, our positive characteristics, true personal power and competence.

Our presence is a synergy of expressions which is hard to grasp. That is why when we meet people, we spend the first few minutes "getting a line" on who they are. We examine each other thoroughly with all our senses. We look, hear, listen, and even smell in order to know how others identify themselves through posture, attitude, scent and appearance. We really would like to be able to circle, sniff, touch and feel each other! Etiquette prevents us from exercising the urge to scan each other from head to toe. Necks tense up and stiffen as we try to hide and stifle this instinct.

We do this natural "checking out" not as a means of judgement, but as a way to create safety for ourselves. Instinctively, we collect sensory and intuitive information and come to a conclusion about an individual. Reaching a sudden estimate of another person may help us to better relate to him or her—an important advantage if we work in sales. Everyone scrutinizes a newcomer—even children do, and they do it best—as a means of establishing who we are in the presence of another person.

In this quick moment of appraisal, we put a

boundary on who we think this person is in order to set the pattern for communication. We make decisions on their capability, status, power, position, background and intelligence. Quite naturally, we adhere to a mini-protocol even in the most insignificant interaction. But when we go no further than summing up basic descriptions of other people, we often leave them feeling underestimated and misunderstood for who they really are. The fact is, they *are* being underestimated.

We are all subjected to similar assessments all the time. Women especially get annoyed if their capabilities and worth are judged by their degree of physical attractiveness. Naomi Wolf clearly demonstrates in *The Beauty Myth* how image is a serious form of miscalculation of women's values and true worth.

Your presence will instantaneously dictate how you appear to others. You have approximately thirty seconds to create a first impression. Every time you meet someone, whether for the first time or hundreth time, the thirty-second syndrome comes into play again. Considering what little time you have to express yourself in most conversations, it is important that you take these few seconds into full account.

A lawyer once told me: "A jury makes a decision about the guilt or innocence of defendants in the first thirty seconds they walk in the room. It takes the rest of the trial to change that decision."

The only way to change this often unfair, quick appraisal is to project an inner picture that balances with the outer one. You may have the perfect wardrobe and sport flawless makeup, yet you manage to communicate negative messages about yourself. People pick this up and judge it to be true. Regardless of how well you look, the inner picture is broadcast as well. A good wardrobe, hairstyle and grooming alone won't do it.

Image and presence cannot be separated, yet people continually try to do it. They even try to appear to be something other than what they are really thinking and feeling. What you think and feel in your *presence* is a perception of you. It is not what you are, but it is a powerful description which influences your environment. For instance, the woman who appears to all her friends and colleagues to be the perfectly controlled, together person, secretly cries without knowing why. She has mastered how she appears to be, but there is a very real grief eating her up inside.

Somehow, however, the truth is showing. Or the man who appears to be doing everything he should, fulfilling outside expectations, one day wakes up and realizes he hasn't been happy for the past twenty years. Somehow his confusion has been apparent to others, even if not to himself.

Studies reveal that more than 80 percent of our communication is accomplished by appearance, body language, facial expression and tone of voice. Combined, these qualities are a powerful means of getting a desired message across. Unfortunately, this also holds true for expressing "undesired" messages. These are messages that you may or may not be aware of and some of which you may like to eliminate from your subconscious vocabulary. But how can you change unwanted or self-limiting messages? And, if you do that, will it really change how others perceive you? Will this really change and enhance your image? The answer is a resounding "Yes."

In order to empower your image it is necessary to create harmony in the inner picture, which is revealed regardless of whether you want to exhibit it or not. You can consciously change the inner picture of yourself with skills as practical as picking out the right suit. One of the first things to do is to go within to examine the limits you have set for yourself. These confining limits are based on your conditioning as a child and can be eliminated to give you wider horizons in which to express your true self. This action does wonders for your body language. Releasing the conditioning of negative thoughts and feelings is a sure way to establish clear and direct communication with others. Instead of being self-conscious, we can be consciously changing. Our image supports and reinforces the importance of the messages we convey as we come into contact with people and establish relationships with them—in our professional as well as our private lives. We can revitalize our image and empower our communication with personal presence.

You may have a high self-esteem, a strong inner worth, know your life purpose and are even on your way to accomplishing it. However, if you do not bring that inner picture to your outer appearance you will misrepresent yourself. Your image will be an obstacle to your communication instead of an empowerment. It will act as a block to your true self, and others will know this in the way you look, sound, talk and act.

What can we do about it? How can the power of

presence communicate our real selves? What gives one person more presence than another? Is it the way they look, talk, listen, move, think, act—or all of the above? These questions will be answered in this book. Can *anyone* achieve the *power of personal presence?*

Yes. Anyone can enjoy an effective presence—CEO, housewife, student, secretary, manager, displaced homemaker or sales agent. It requires going to the heart of image, learning what it is and how you can attain and maintain it. Enhancing your outer image will help to communicate the real you, but empowering your *presence* will make you believable, because it *will be* true.

THE SYNERGY
OF PERSONAL PRESENCE

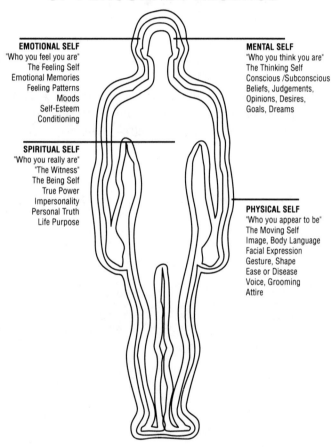

EMOTIONAL SELF
"Who you feel you are"
The Feeling Self
Emotional Memories
Feeling Patterns
Moods
Self-Esteem
Conditioning

MENTAL SELF
"Who you think you are"
The Thinking Self
Conscious /Subconscious
Beliefs, Judgements,
Opinions, Desires,
Goals, Dreams

SPIRITUAL SELF
"Who you really are"
"The Witness"
The Being Self
True Power
Impersonality
Personal Truth
Life Purpose

PHYSICAL SELF
"Who you appear to be"
The Moving Self
Image, Body Language
Facial Expression
Gesture, Shape
Ease or Disease
Voice, Grooming
Attire

CHAPTER 2

Personal Presence

"Work harder to become something than to get something."
Axel Fredelholm

"I know of no more encouraging fact than the unquestionable ability of man to elevate his life by a conscious endeavor."
Henry David Thoreau

Personal presence is the "true state of being" that develops as a result of harmonious communication between the thinking self (psychological), feeling self (emotional), moving self (physical) and being self (spiritual).

A synergy of self occurs when all thoughts and emotions (conscious, subconscious, and unconscious) and aspects of the body (health, five senses, movement and appearance) interlink with a positive awareness that allows the free expression of your true power from the spiritual self, which is *who you really are.*

Look at the illustration on page 10 which shows the interrelationship of the four selves and personal presence. These four aspects are in constant fluctuation and interaction. They are each interdependently in commonciation with each other as well as interacting with other people. When these four are harmoniously balanced, you are in a state of powerful personal presence that is experienced on all levels.

The physical self, emotional self and mental self are parts of the *personality* that can be thought of as *assets*. Assets are qualities and commodities that are constantly changing and can be shaped, directed and improved. The spiritual self is your *impersonality,* an eternal essence that is an unchanging principle within the changing mind, body and feelings. The spiritual self is your wise and knowing self—a constant self-*worth.*

When you are fully present and act with true power, you are more than your personal assets, *You Are A Team.* The team players are your *body,* your *mind,* your *emotions* and your *spirit.* As a team, each self must be cooperating with the other and focused toward the same goal. This is important to your every decision and choice.

Think about a time when:

... you made a decision based solely on physical or material attraction without regard for the whole person. Did something go wrong?

... you made a decision based solely on career opportunity without regard to your other inner voices. Honestly, were you disappointed with the job?

... you made a decision or acted with raw

emotion? What happened in your communication? Did you create harmony or conflict?

... you intellectually rationalized your way through a decision without regard to your feelings? Did you really circumvent your emotions or were they eventually disclosed?

... you made a decision purely based on financial data. Did an imbalance of some kind show up later ?

... the image you projected did not reflect your true competence? Did your appearance hold you back?

... you decided to trust someone without noticing your intuitive voice that said not to? Were the consequences disempowering?

You create from an inner state all the time. When one of your four selves—any member of the team—is left out of a decision, then an imbalance is created, because your state of being at the time you made the decision was imbalanced. These states are both visible and invisible communicators that are detected by everyone around you. Each team member is an expression other people can see, feel and perceive. It is quite apparent when one part of yourself is out of balance.

What You Think And Feel You Will Project

The key to achieving personal presence requires that you go to the source of your verbal and non-verbal communication and to closely observe how this center actually generates your presence. Most people are apprehensive about exploring this inner center because they would rather deny and hide from their thoughts and feelings. They disregard what is going on inside of them because they believe it is unimportant. Yet thoughts and feelings are major components of conscious change and empowerment, and are powerful enough to create a kinetic movement that is subconsciously detectable by other people—they will know what you are thinking and feeling. The body does not lie. Its movements interpret the state of your inner activities. The mind can deny, but the body cannot.

A participant—I shall call her Leslie—who attended one of my training sessions was impeccably dressed and obviously had the money to buy whatever she wanted. She participated in the first exercise in which members of the group took thirty seconds to appraise each other as they stood alone silently in front of the room. The instant assessments were made anonymously and given to her to open later when she arrived home. Leslie was amazed to learn that over half of the class perceived her to be insecure. Although her outer appearance had all the right qualities and she did not stand with her shoulders slumping and hands fidgeting, she subtly communicated her state of inner insecurity.

The group picked up her signals immediately. Leslie's thoughts had created a field of energy from the source of her inner self that shouted insecurity and self-limiting thoughts.

What you are thinking and feeling will be revealed
to others whether you are conscious of it or not.

"As a man thinketh, so is he."
Socrates

I remember the president of a company who came to me for help in refining his inner and outer image so that he could project a presence of credibility, confidence and ease. We worked on uncovering his subconscious conditioning and disempowering beliefs, and observed how his specific attitudes affected his personal presence and communication. We began a process which would last over several weeks of changing negative qualities into empowering personal values. Soon, his revitalized confidence and his strengthened assertiveness soared. He felt powerful and sure of himself.

That good feeling lasted until he had lunch with Mr. B. who had more experience, was wealthier and enjoyed a more powerful social position. My client became fidgety, uncomfortable and projected his uncertainties to the person he wanted to impress. When I asked him what the emotions behind his discomfort were, he looked at me quizzically and said he never thought about his emotions. But true to its law, the body projected his feelings and emotions regardless of my client's intent to put his best image forward. This event was quite revealing to him. He began to understand the power of presence on a deep level. My client had more work ahead of him.

Changing the outer appearance is the focus of the majority of people, since it is the most obvious type of transformation. It is also the easiest. Most people are more concerned with their appearance than they are with their health. They do not know about the deeper levels of relaxation that are attainable. Many people, especially in business, do not acknowledge their emotions or talk about their feelings. Others are not conscious of their everyday self-talk and have not learned to focus their thoughts. Many have completely forgotten their spiritual connection which shows in their eyes, image, body language, thinking and actions. It is crucial to personal presence to have all four parts of yourself working together simultaneously.

Lack of fulfillment occurs whenever you give up part of yourself for another person or another aspect of yourself. Perhaps you stop exercising your body in order to work harder mentally, or you repress your feelings in order to avoid conflict and change, or deny your thoughts in order to sabotage your success and happiness, or maybe you ignore your spirit in order to avoid spiritual awareness.

We are much happier, more fulfilled and effective when we become aware of the fact that we are *whole* beings. We fare much better in life if we *sense* this wholeness as well as *know, trust* and *breathe* in it.

When you are working as a team, each member has an awareness of its importance to the bottom line experience of the whole unit. Each team member is a conscious and contributing factor to the process and end result. As on any team, the process as well as the result is equally important, because the process affects the quality of the result. We may have a vision of a goal of what we want to feel, act, look and be but the task is to create that vision and reach that goal.

Let's look at the specifics of the four selves—
Your Personal Team:

Physical Self
This self includes two parts:
A. Body Image: Shape, size, grooming, clothing
    (color, texture, style, accessories, etc.) skin,
    hair and face appearance.
B. Body Consciousness: Health, ease and dis-ease,
    muscular tension and awareness, movement,
    body language, posture, facial expression, five
    senses (smell, touch, taste, sight, sound) and
    energy system (chakras, energy flow,
    meridians).

Emotional Self
A. Emotional response system and reactive
    conditioning, emotional memory patterns
B. Emotions: Joy/grief, anger/peace, courage/fear,
    love/hate,compassion/judgement,
    pride/shame, innocence/guilt,
    disappointment/enthusiasm, sarcasm/
    encouragement, regard/prejudice, trust/distrust,
    honesty/dishonesty, etc.

Mental Self
A. The Mind: The conscious mind, subconscious
    mind and the unconscious mind.
B. Thoughts : All memories, dreams, visions,
    observations, opinions, beliefs, perceptions,
    self-talk and mind chatter. Together these form
    mental paradigms which are either building

blocks or stumbling blocks based on your conditioning.

Spiritual Self

A. The Witness, the Observer. The true Self. Your superconscious being. Inner teacher and guide. Spirit. Source of authentic power.

B. State of Inner Silence: Self-fulfillment, rich inner life, wisdom, intuition, *super*consciousness, heightened awareness, equanimity. The Witness is an observer, ever ready to offer insight, intuition and support, but never controls the situation (unless you yield to it).

The external and the internal are two different directions which can exist in perfect harmony. When the external reflects the internal true self, the body, mind and emotions are working as a harmonious team creating the synergy of personal presence.

Claiming personal presence is the process of uncovering, recovering and discovering your true self—by enhancing your *persona*. The Latin word for personality is persona, which means mask. The persona of the self is comprised of the three masks of personality—masks that we use to interact with the world.

The development of persona is the key to consciously becoming real. We must go within and discover the *unmasked self,* the *im*-persona, or *impersonality*. Only when we know this self, and let it be the source of our nature, our habits, our thinking and feeling, will we understand ourselves, understand others and be understood.

It is necessary to take off each mask of the persona and observe, understand, even love it. Then the masks of your mind, body and emotions respond with a flow of communication in harmony because they feel recognized and worthy. Even that part of the self that is engaged in an unwanted, unhealthy habit will feel embraced with understanding and safe to let the habit of thought or action go with ease.

This part of you that holds the mask in your hand is the Observer, the Spiritual Self that I call the Witness.

The Witness quietly waits for the persona to become authentic. It is natural to have an innate yearning to express your authenticity, your unique presence; it is also your birthright. Before you are understood and seen for who you really are, you must first experience self-discovery. When you understand the masks of your persona, you can honor them for who and what they have represented for you. You can take them off, one by one, and mold, shape and shine them so that they are clear. You must consciously *clarify* the masks.

Clarissa Estés defines persona in *Women Who Run With The Wolves*, to be "not simply a mask to hide behind, but rather a presence which eclipses the mundane personality—a persona that is a signal of rank, virtue, character and authority."

As long as we have a body, mind and emotions we have masks of the persona. It is our duty to hone and shape our masks to represent ourselves to the best of our ability and to demonstrate our traits of character, intentions, purpose and values.

The masks of persona are not something to dispose of, but to enhance and form as clear expressions of our real self. To do this, we must address ourselves for who we are completely.

The target is to achieve the five characteristics of personal presence.

The Five Characteristics of Personal Presence

Clarity: Clarity is a distinctiveness about your presence. You can feel it and have a look of straightforwardness, free of hidden agendas and old masks from the past that you are trying to work out on the innocent people around you. Clarity involves shaping your masks to reflect your inner self. That requires wiping and clearing the mirror that you look into, until you see who you really are.

Communication: Presence is the key to communication, both verbal and nonverbal. You cannot respond to people unless you really hear what they are saying—not just the words, but their true meaning. This is a learned skill. Some people have memories of not being seen or heard, and they find it challenging to stay *present* to hear others. Presence enables you to listen authentically.

Confidence: Confidence is the memory of liking oneself in the presence of others. This provides a foundation on which new experiences can be anchored as positive learning blocks which keep expanding and strengthening the base of self-esteem. Confidence can be acquired with memory-building techniques and self-awareness practices.

Credibility: Credibility is the spectrum of a reliable set of beliefs and personal values that, through your persona, extends beyond yourself and has a positive influence on other people. Values, personal truth, life purpose and self-worth contribute to the attribute of credibility.

Caring: Caring is sharing yourself, your true self, with others. Holding your real self back, so that you can get ahead hasn't done much in the past, has it? When you come into the heart of your image, your true self, your purpose extends to others with the sole intention of good, without thought of reward. The act of true caring is empowering to yourself and those around you.

• • •

Your presence embodies all your expressed and repressed thoughts and feelings as well as your dreams and aspirations. It also conveys your life purpose and personal values. Your ability to project personal presence and personal power is greatly determined by the roles that you agree to play and your conditioning—learned thoughts, feelings, and behaviors. That is why it is important to understand your past and present beliefs and to *unlearn* negative conditioning, and to build on that foundation in order to achieve lasting and fulfilling change. All of these subjects affect personal presence and will be addressed in this book.

In Part Two, specific practices are given to assist you in achieving the power of personal presence. I have separated the how-to section so that you can easily find specific areas of interest and refer to them any time.

CHAPTER 3

Physical Presence

"A fair exterior is a silent recommendation."
Publius Syrus, Maxims, 1st Century B. C.

As we meet and greet new people, our physical presence is the main communicator. Our body image makes the first impression; secondly, our body language speaks for us. Next, our tone of voice conveys its messages. Then our sense of hearing (how are we listening?) and touch (is touching natural and comfortable?) come into play. Finally, we are perceived by the words we speak. Any one of these can overide an impression created by the other. The most radiant smile can reduce the impact of poor clothing choices, or the kindest gesture can help erase the impression of helplessness. Likewise, the tone of voice can make the most attractive person seem ugly. An inappropriate body contact can make the most charming person into a rogue. All these aspects of verbal and non-verbal communication make up the total *physical* presence.

Image symbolizes a rite of passage in society. The CEO, the operations manager, the young mother of two, the attorney, the temporary secretary, the beauty consultant, the sales rep: All have a look that marks their identity.

We feel more confident not only when we look better, but because we are sure of where we *belong*. That sense of belonging to a group is so absolutely imperative to human adaptation that a person will seek out those with whom he feels comfortable even if the environment is destructive. People go to great lengths to establish their identity.

Image influences our identity much more than we like to admit. Our appearance affects our lives as much as our lives affect our appearance. A *personal best* image is an asset that can open many doors. When you look your best, you become an asset to your environment—the company you work for, the community in which you live or the organization in which you volunteer time.

A true image transformation is a partnership between the tangible enhancement of the appearance and the intangible experience of empowerment. Your outer image can empower your inner image by achieving your personal best image, which is an asset. Reaching your human potential is a process of building your assets and putting them to work for you. Your assets may get you a higher starting wage in a new company, a faster promotion or simply get the job over a dozen other applicants. It is of value to develop and use as many assets as you can.

The more that you *look* capable of facilitating a

team project, organizing and hosting a large dinner party, planning a company event, negotiating a profitable deal, meeting a deadline, or consoling a friend, the more capable you will *feel.*

This does NOT mean that you must have a specific height and body weight in order to look and project that capability. On the contrary. Believing that you must conform to precarious social standards of body shape and size is like being a work horse driven in the fields while wearing blinders; you can't see where you have been or where you are going, and you have lost a mind of your own. To nurture such a disempowering belief has no value other than to punish yourself and those around you. This is not a characteristic of personal presence.

Some of the most capable, powerful, significant contributors to our society have been men and women who defy the so-called norm that the fashion/beauty industry promotes. And some of the most beautiful women I have known are incapable of seeing themselves as limited by something as superficial as body shape. The most disempowering part of being a petite man or a wide-hipped woman is finding the best-fitting clothes. That's it. Anyone, no matter their size and shape has a personal best image *now.* It is merely a question of designing your look to project your best.

Your image design indicates how you feel about yourself, and sometimes your worth. Grooming is very important. This can express how worthy you think and feel you are. Your image speaks volumes about where you have been, and where you plan to go in the future. It cannot give you worth, but it can help you *project* it.

A company once sent to me a new account executive with an allowance to help her acquire a complete wardrobe upgrade because they wanted to get her "out there."

A manager came to me for guidance to choose her professional wardrobe and within a month she was promoted with a raise in pay. She increased her stature in the company by looking more polished, put-together and professional, which matched her true competence.

A doctor hired me to arrange a new progressive wardrobe while he worked diligently at toning his body. His payoff was an easier fit in his jackets and confidence in his appearance while he treated his patients and socialized with his peers.

All three clients increased their assets.

Image is the immediate, first impression. The image or facade of the body is formed with color, shape, texture and proportion. The body itself has all of these elements, as do the image design of your wardrobe, makeup, grooming and hair. Everything in the world of form has color, shape, texture and proportion.

Physical presence demands you have an awareness of your most harmonious and effective image design. You are aware of what makes you look poor, mediocre, good and excellent. You are able to effectively use your image to create choice and freedom in your life, instead of obstacles to your growth. Your image empowers you and synchronizes who you are—your work and your relationships. The look itself is not distracting to the real you. It is enhancing.

Physical presence has a very real purpose. You can communicate your moods, your goals, your values. It can simply give others a clue to what you are up to presently. You develop an awareness of how you are perceived when you wear a suit or a sweater, walk around the office with your jacket on or off, buttoned or unbuttoned. With each and every detail of your clothing, you are making a statement as to how you plan the day or evening to proceed.

Even though body image is such an obvious form of self-projection, many powerful men and women still choose to ignore it, perhaps because it is so obvious. Your identity, personality and style are essential to the quality of self-expression. To deny or limit yourself to an image that is not your personal best, is not only detrimental to your self awareness, but to your relationships. People will be able to detect your discomfort with the way you look. Others may assume that you are not true to yourself, or worse, do not know how to be.

Sometimes people feel guilty when they buy something that will improve their appearance. They feel so unworthy of it that they end up with a look that is not flattering to them—makeup, hairstyles, clothing which are either unsuited to them or make them fade into the background. This non-verbal language is saying, "I don't like myself." "Don't look at me." "I'm scared." "I don't like my body" "I don't care about my body" and "I don't deserve to look attractive."

For most people, a lifetime of exposure to advertising, and advice from friends and family, coupled with an undeveloped eye for style and the inability to shop efficiently, leaves them confused and bewildered. This confusion is expensive to the consumer. It is a poor use of time and money and is a neglect of personal resources and attributes.

It takes the same amount of time to shop for the best personal style as it does to end up with a humdrum, mediocre look. Many shoppers buy clothing, hairstyles and accessories that are just plain wrong in color, shape and texture.

In the same way, many people carry around a negative or unflattering inner picture of themselves that has been formed over the years. They wear this inner picture as surely as any garment. That inner picture easily translates to appearance. Their choice of appearance actually sends more messages to *themselves* than they send to others.

Consider the whole picture when you look in the mirror, give a presentation at work, or chauffeur children around town. Your presentation to others will affect the level of satisfaction you attain on a daily level. Your relationship with yourself, your appearance, your children, your boss, your customers—literally everyone—is important to fully enjoy your life.

Image design is the easiest phase of transformation. The refinement of visual appearance is devised with creative wit in coordinating the elements of form and function. All aspects of color, style, personal taste and lifestyle come into play when designing a look that will best compliment you. The result of such an endeavor is the creation of your personal style, style signature or look. In this way, you are a fashion stylist, the final step to bringing vitality to the art of fashion. When you are wearing your personal best style, you are making a statement—a very *loud* statement about yourself.

Image works for you when you are silent.

When we are *present* in our bodies, we exude a sense of really being there, grounded, so to speak. The body flows in graceful, poised movements as a whole unit with a marked coordination and sensory awareness. There are no jerky, uncoordinated moves from the various parts of the body which give the impression they are unaware of what the mind intends for them to do. The mind/body communication, or the mind/body connection, has been recognized lately as a major factor in maintaining physical health and well-being. If you are present physically, you look like you are comfortable walking around inside of your body and have a genuinely friendly and warm personal regard for it.

Your body is graceful and enjoys a state of good health and healing. There are no "numb" places in this state—such as people who cannot feel their ice cold hands and feet. If you are present physically, you can sense and receive messages from your body. Your body becomes a channel of heightened awareness through which your intuition communicates to let you know what is happening around you. You have keen senses, and you use them. The mind/body connection is at peak performance when your mind is listening to your body, and your body responds to the mind, as is the case with athletes.

A large part of physical presence involves a relatively young science called kinesics. Kinesics is the study of body movement in relation to speech. Our body language is the message that we send out with our stance, gesture, expressions, and body boundaries. It can include both conscious and unconscious movements that communicate emotional messages to those around you.

Your body movement reveals to the trained eye what I call "body history." You can tell exactly what a person is feeling now and much of his past by observing his body movement. The slightest adjustment in body alignment can greatly affect your feelings. Try this: Get yourself in the body alignment of someone you know. In short, imitate them. Stay in that position for one minute. You will actually begin to "feel" the way they are feeling on the inside. If you tell them this, they may object, because they may be numb to their own feelings and thoughts. Do this several times while walking, standing or running. If you imitate someone who is graceful and aligned, you will feel a sense of confidence and even power. If you do not think you are worthy of this, or have a confused picture of what humility looks like, if you think slumped shoulders convey humbleness, then you may not initially feel comfortable when standing in alignment.

A young mother participated in one of my dynamic relaxation exercise classes. When she attained a fully aligned position, it was a new and peculiar sensation for her. I asked her what she felt when she stood in alignment. She responded, "This is how I would stand if I was a proud person." The kinesthetic experience of standing correctly gave her an immediate *sense* of self-worth. She needed to claim that sensation, that state, as a natural daily condition.

An adjustment in alignment can be powerfully transforming. A slight change can open up the space for the release of previously unknown, hidden emotional memory needing to be released. That is movement therapy and the release of body history or *physically living in the past.* Using the body as a grounding focus is a valid form of therapeutic change today and one of the most powerful components to clearing the past.

In one of my private counseling sessions on movement I worked with a client who suffered from neck pain even though there was no external cause for it. As we worked with moving his body energy connecting his head and heart, the cause of the pain revealed itself. An old resentment towards his dominating father who was still a "pain in the neck" to him, literally manifested in his body. His body was still living in the past. He cleared up the past, and greatly improved his presence.

> *We empower our presence by clearing up the past in our bodies.*

When you have your body in the room, you usually think that your are physically present. However, there are people who enter a place and remain invisible at will just by their lack of expression. This may be excellent when you wish to go unnoticed, but it is devastating when you really want to be seen.

You may feel unwanted, taken for granted or lost. In any case, if others do not notice you, you are doing something wrong. You are not generating enough energy to be noticed, much less spoken to. That is very disempowering.

The invisible person will carefully sidestep objects, just as a waiter avoids disturbing the customers he is waiting on. The invisible person will do this even when not performing a service function. They will adjust themselves rather than adjust their environment to work for them. Women do this unconsciously at work or in a meeting where it is not beneficial to be invisible. This could be a habit learned from the service-oriented nature of jobs women are used to having: nursing, waitressing, home caring, etc. These habits can be unlearned.

Then there are those who are in the room before their body arrives. They simply take up too much space. They may back you into a corner without realizing it, because they are unaware that they are invading your personal body sphere. We all have a natural space that is comfortable to reserve for ourselves and our closest kin and friends. Everyone else can back off. Honoring the boundaries that other people set for themselves is very important.

A story was told to me of a gentleman who was interviewing for a senior position in a company. The president took him to lunch in what seemed to be the yes-you-have-it-in-the-bag luncheon. When he did not get the job, he asked why. The response shocked him. During lunch he had excused himself from the table and neglected to replace his chair securely out of the moving space of the waiters. He did not get the job due to his lack of awareness and courtesy to other people. This behavior, however unconscious, displayed a lack for respect for the boundaries and personal safety for those in his presence. It really pays to know and respect what is happening in the space around you.

Voices, too, have a definite presence. The tone of voice can be the key to establishing great rapport or it can be so distracting that the meaning of the spoken words is literally stripped away. You can excite or soothe, persuade or disgust, attract or rebuff someone simply with the presence of your voice.

Speaking with presence can be summed up with a look at the classic movie *My Fair Lady*. Diction and tone of voice were keys to Liza Dolittle's ability to fool everyone into believing she was a member of royalty. She was a woman who climbed the ladder of the caste system simply by changing her physical presence in image, body language, tone, rhythm and diction of speech.

A friend told me the story of admiring an elegant woman from a distance for over a week during her stay at a luxury spa in California. She was appalled one day when she heard the woman speak. The chic woman's strong accent accompanied by incorrect grammar were enough to blow the elegant impression to smithereens, and with it the desire to meet the offending voice.

Not all accents are distracting. The soft and gentle inflection of regional origin can be as appealing as its cuisine, customs and native flora. However, improper grammar, a monotone rhythm or inarticulate diction sound bad no matter what the accent. It is not the accent, it is the *entire rhythm of voice that counts*.

A sage once said: "We are born with two ears and one mouth, so we should be listening twice as much as we speak."

If we indeed are good listeners, our communication improves greatly. People often hear actual words, but fail to listen to the meaning behind the words. Perhaps they simply do not want to know what the other person means, and since they do not want to be direct, or are afraid of speaking out, the message gets lost.

With true physical presence, listening is an action. People who feel that to listen is to be passively hearing someone else are not actively listening, but only waiting for others to take a breath so that they can cut in to get their own opinion across. Often, this opinion is not a response at all, but a reaction to their anxiety in communication. Have you ever watched someone disengage and plan in her mind what she is going to say next?

Then if you say, "You aren't listening," she will repeat every word as if proving that she had been listening. This is an annoying form of interaction that creates anxiety. Studies have shown that when you fail to listen with presence, the other person's blood pressure rises. The next time this happens to you, notice what your own body feels like and you will sense the anxiety yourself. If you react with the same lack of presence, you will notice how tired you are at the end of the conversation due to the nervous strain. Listening with presence is healthy for you.

When we listen with physical presence, our bodies are doing the majority of the listening. Your body can become so sensitive to the feelings and thoughts of others that it is an excellent instrument for hearing the meaning behind the spoken words. Since most people do not share what they really mean directly, this is a powerful means of listening. You do not have to mimic someone else's body language to do it. The mind is silent, and your body listens. It is a marvelous gift and can be learned by anyone. Babies are experts at it. Basically, the awareness of listening is a relearning process.

Be aware that your body is capable of sensing if someone is telling the truth. The skin is an excellent detector of stimuli and information coming from the environment. What actually happens is that you have reached a state of presence with no judgement, and the Witness gives you signals and clues through body sensation. When you listen to your body talk to you, instinctively, you know how to act or respond in a given situation. The body cannot lie, and you can trust it.

It is a common mistake to engage in negative self-talk about our bodies. With physical presence, you will rarely say or think negative things about your body just to be saying something. In the English language we have adopted an array of phrases that are biolinguistic. According to how we refer to our bodies in common everyday language, we do not esteem them in the way we do our hearts and spirit.

Some common phrases are:

"Get off my back"—"I stuck my neck

out on that one"—"It made my skin crawl"—"Tight-lipped"—"I put my foot in my mouth"—"Stiff-necked"—"To lose face"—"Weak-kneed"—" Hard-headed"—"Spineless".

There are hundreds more expressions which refer to parts of our body that have negative connotations. Phrases like these do nothing to help you maintain physical presence, because your body simply hears what you say and think. It listens to you as much as it listens to others. Just as our minds can listen to messages from our bodies, so our bodies listen to what we say and think about it. Our bodies do not appreciate it when we denigrate their marvelous functions and abilities.

It is unfortunate that we do not have many uplifting phrases about our bodies. The language we use is void of expressions to celebrate our bodies, as if people aren't ready and willing to feel intense pleasure, openness of heart, extreme aliveness, spiritual peace, well-being and deep relaxation. In fact, when people use uplifting expressions, they are often viewed as something weird or even mystical.

People in every walk of life have experienced days of being mentally *off*—that feeling of *just not really being here*. They find themselves suddenly aware that they do not feel their bodies and that they have been *off* thinking of the past or dreaming of the future.

This is an indication that your body is being ignored—you don't hear it. Your body is actually speaking to you and giving you information and guidance about the best way to work things out. You may suddenly wake up and feel pain because you ignored earlier signals. This pain may have been there for some time, but now you can feel it. What do you think your body has been trying to tell you all this time?

Physical presence displays a healthy demeanor that is the result of a lifestyle of self-care. Exercise, proper foods, relaxation are imperative. The choices you make about food and drink are readily apparent in the way your skin, hair and eyes appear. There are no beauty products available that will cover or distract from an unhealthy countenance or deliver the radiance of true honest feelings.

The way you face the world is important to your presence. People sometimes try to "keep face." They are trained to hide themselves behind the accepted expression of what they call smiling. But it is not smiling. A graciousness so well accomplished on the outside can sometimes grow a hard shell around it that not only protects from the outside but will keep you from knowing yourself on the inside. It puts up a false front to a lot of people, and the smile is no longer a smile, but a grin. The grin sometimes looks strained and practiced. This is referred to as the "grin and bear it" look. The disconcerting thing about this is that you can sometimes find yourself in a room full of people who are "grinning and bearing it." This insincerity breeds false grace and it is quite noticeable. If you manipulate yourself in this way, without coming to terms with your real self within, you will not achieve an effective personal presence.

In one of my workshops, a whole group of participants was surprised when one of the leaders was unwilling to honor her true feelings. She had to make a concerted effort to manipulate her demeanor in order to hide her emotional discomfort. By trying to "keep face," she only exacerbated the display of her fears and insecurities. This led some of her colleagues to distrust her and question her leadership skills.

Axel Fredenholm said, "When you seek the truth, be yourself entirely, without pretense. There is no facial mask so skillfully constructed and so carefully worn that it cannot be detected."

Your personal presence demands a willingness to be honest and open with others. The degree to which you are willing to see your inner magnificence beyond the facade of makeup and clothing, is the degree to which you will know yourself.

Know how you are *facing* the world.

In the book, *The Art of Joyful Living*, Swami Rama says, "There can be a perennial and real smile on your face all the time. To achieve that you need to have a clear concept about the meaning of life—then you will start functioning on a different and deeper level, and you will begin to enjoy life."

This joy radiates through your personal presence.

CHAPTER 4

Emotional Presence

"Courage is the price that life exacts for granting peace."
Amelia Earhart

When you are present emotionally, you are free of agendas, cleansed of emotional backlog from the past—and it shows. You feel fresh and ready to respond to others from the *Now*—today, not yesterday. Your emotional buttons are not easily pushed. In fact, the only way to get rid of emotional buttons is to heal them with conscious release work. You can relax and let go of tension easily because you have left old resentments and other emotional ballast behind. This action frees you up and makes you look much better. Your presence becomes more alive. You look capable, confident and trustworthy.

Positive emotions have an extraordinary affect on our image—they are life-giving and rejuvenate our very being. They balance our inner selves, slow down the aging process and improve every phase of our lives.

The emotional presence of acceptance, courage, innocence, joy, gratitude and compassion are the centering feelings of different levels of love. They replace negative emotions such as denial, fear, guilt/shame, grief, anger and judgement/prejudice. When you erase the negative, the positive emerges from deep within the center of your being—and it is very exciting. Positive emotions look great on you when you wear them.

Courage is the fountain of energy that opens you to the full experience of emotional presence. Courage is required to begin the process of releasing painful emotional memories. Courage is a leading characteristic of persons who are not afraid to *feel deeply*. They do not avoid their feelings, but through courage have learned to change the negative into the positive. Courage is strong of heart and mind, and is easily seen in your speech, actions and body language.

You do not have to feel courage if you never take risks.

Erica Jong said, "The trouble is, if you don't risk anything, you risk even more." People who react to life from a state of fear instead of courage are depressed, uncertain and veiled in clouds of doubt and worry. They are afraid of seeking their own answers and avoid the unknown. Worst of all, they shun change, and change is what is happening all the time.

Courage precedes all positive change. Courage has the face of a leader, willing to forge ahead undaunted by setbacks and the possibility of failure. It strengthens faith in winning and is a proactive approach to change. Courage is silent strength that acknowledges the challenge, dares to remove it, solve it, jump over it or go around it. It is a smile when life is down, a boost of energy when facing a setback and the willingness to stay on track in times of turmoil.

Courage is standing your ground in the face of adversity and in front of those who would prefer to keep you "in your place", where they mistakenly think you would best serve them. Courage has the dignity of silent power and a deep knowing, and is expressed through resolute actions. Direct eye contact, purposeful motions, grounded stance and an aligned body are the physical distinctions of courage. Courage shows up in your eyes with its message of dignity and perseverance when others give up. It fills your vision with power and empowers others.

Acceptance is an opening up and accepting of reality and establishing personal truth. People who have dealt with acceptance are easy to talk to. They understand depth of feeling and have learned to recognize when life is out of kilter.

Acceptance is open, safe and ready to let you be who you are. It is a love of self that rubs off on those around you. The act of accepting shows on the face: The eyes are soft and glowing, facial muscles are relaxed. Your countenance expresses warmth, understanding and reflects a sense of ease. You have passion and sincerity because you have faced your own weaknesses and are open to accept them in others. Your presence is grounded, centered and approachable.

Innocence is the inner exuberant, intelligent child and has nothing to do with naivete. It is the gift of serenity and selfless pride that shines on your face when you have let go of guilt and shame. Innocence is like cleansing yourself from the inside out, and radiates friendliness, approval and acceptance. Innocence is a state of feeling free, not being self-conscious and wrong, but honest and right. You are light, fun and creative. You create a place where life is simple and pleasing. You have merged with your inner child and you truly feel self-love. You do not use guilt and disapproval as a motivator. You empower others with your freedom of choice.

Joy is the energy of radiance, ease and laughter. Your eyes are clear and strikingly full of life. Your body movements are free, natural, alive and graceful. Your whole being flows and glows with an inviting openness. Joy is uplifting, yet calming, enthusiastic, while relaxing, enduring and strong. It too, is hopeful and life-giving.

Joy erases wrinkles and worry lines and turns them into lines of smiles and laughter. It is a grand gift and is contagious and attractive. You're forever young and make those around wish they were full of joy, too. Joy keeps good company.

Gratitude expresses thanksgiving for all your gifts whether they be tangible or intangible. There is never a time in personal growth when there is no room for gratitude. You can even be thankful for finally beginning to release the anger and shame from the past.

It's no use being angry that you are angry, or sad that you are grieving. Gratitude helps move out these emotions more quickly. Gratitude opens your heart and mind to see the good in the world, even at challenging and confusing times. Practice it everyday. It softens your demeanor and allows love to flow in.

Gratitude warms your hands, lightens your thoughts, and allows you to let go. It lifts depression, increases your positive outlook and prolongs life. It helps you overlook any unkindness, and makes you appreciate kindness shown to you.

Compassion improves your image beyond your wildest imagination. It is the essential quality of true leadership. Compassion for others stems from your ability to forgive yourself. Only if you have compassion for yourself can you give to others. Giving from guilt brings pain, giving of yourself out of compassion brings positive transformation. Discovering the power of compassion is the truest meaning of a Win-Win approach to life.

Compassion dispels false sincerity, and eliminates the "grin and bear it" look. Compassion makes you an excellent listener, which is the golden key to intimacy. It helps you to listen and to speak only when others are ready to listen to you. It lets you be still and wait your turn. You look powerful and sincere at the same time.

These qualities simply cannot be expressed through image alone. It won't do any good to be impeccably dressed as long as you still resent someone or something from the past and carry it around inside your body—say, your shoulders, neck or hands. Holding onto the past is a sure sign of "stuffing" it.

Unfortunately, if you are in the habit of stuffing negative emotions, you also stuff the good ones—like enthusiasm, joy, compassion, etc. The body, like the subconscious mind, does not differentiate between positive and negative, but stores everything you offer. Releasing the accumulation of emotional garbage is easier than people think. The main requirement is the courage to feel and experience compassion for yourself.

If you are emotionally not present, you will feel constant waves of emotion emerging from within which continue to distort your image. It is wise to get the assistance of a qualified counselor who can help you *relieve* the pressure by *reliving* the events that caused the disturbance in the first place. Alice Miller has said that problems cannot be solved with words, but only through experience, not merely corrective experience, but through a reliving of early experience. John Bradshaw, the renowned therapist of inner child work agrees with this statement when he says,"You can't heal what you can't feel."

There is an abundance of holistic healing approaches that include inner child, breath awareness, movement psychology and transpersonal therapy. Processes such as these allow you to erase unwanted memory emotions and reframe them with empowering insights. Precious time is spent going over and over in your mind a painful situation from the past which cannot be changed. It takes even more precious energy to repress and deny it. Recreating and changing the past is impossible, so why keep it alive?

Emotional presence occurs when you are emotionally *responding,* not reacting. When you harbor old anger, then you are reacting to the past, often with greater intensity than the circumstances require. The slightest comment can set off a barrage of negative self-talk, or mental rehash of blame and justification for your feelings. You will tend to blow situations and feelings out of proportion. You may even read into a conversation all your own internal fears. This is how some people punish themselves—by carrying around past resentments which are meaningless in the present. This is disempowering, and you cannot respond in a positive way if you are in a reactive mode.

Continuing research projects on how negative emotions affect the state of health in people are conducted in hospitals and universities every day. These studies have brought to light the fact that our emotions affect our health, and hence, the way we look. You need to care for your body and emotional states. Bernie Siegel, author of *Love, Medicine and Miracles,* says, "Your body knows what is going on in your life."

A common culprit is stress. Stress affects our health, our relationships, our work—in fact it touches and taints every aspect of life, and becomes noticeable in our appearances. The medical profession acknowledges that stress generates discomfort and disease. Research has shown that 70 percent of all visits to a physician's office are for stress-related problems. Juliet Schor, in *The Overworked American* states that "Time off due to stress related ailments is increasing rapidly in the work culture."

Stress may not always be a product of a serious problem, but can be a delightful event—such as the stress of falling in love, getting a promotion, preparing for a big trip, building our dream home or winning the lottery. We have come to view stress as a troublemaker and define it as negative.

Whether a situation is stressful or not is determined by the *reaction* of the underlying emotions. Feelings of fear, anger, sorrow, guilt, and shame make up the emotional bottom line to stress. In you fall in love, for instance, and begin to feel strung out with the stress of it all, then it is not the love that is causing stress, but some other emotions that are clamoring for attention. It could be fear. Being in love can produce the fear of abandonment or loss of love, freedom or independence. The fear is stressful, not love.

When you have cleared up your emotional past, your levels of stress are greatly reduced. You are able to empower and support others emotionally who want to clear up their own fears, instead of project them onto you. You cannot help them reduce stress if you do not know how to do it yourself.

All negative emotions can be traced to some form of fear. Most people experience some kind of fear—men and women alike. *The Course in Miracles*, a book of sublime dimensions, contributes the following thought, "The decision to wake (become emotionally present) is the reflection of the will to love, since all healing involves replacing fear with love."

Fear affects everything if you do not recognize and eliminate it. It generates all kinds of disempowering behaviors. Actions, such as those following, reflect internal states of fear that lack presence.

Avoiding success or a promotion;

Harming your physical health with poor eating or abuse;

Holding back your attractiveness;

Avoiding or sabotaging a good relationship;

Passing up opportunities to be heard and seen;

Focusing on negative feedback and diminishing the positive;

Expressing guilt and shame;

Giving up your power to a boss, mate, friend or child;

Deflecting your worth;

Failing to set goals;

Clinging to addictive behavior;

Not acting on your knowledge because it wasn't "your place;"

Denying and withholding the truth;

Staying in an abusive relationship;

Permitting harassment personally, socially or at work;

Being afraid to say no;

Looking to others for approval but not accepting when it is there;

Ignoring your intuition;

Shutting down your feelings;

Harboring archaic prejudices;

Doing everything yourself, not delegating or accepting support;

Being unable to take constructive criticism.

It is important to not simply give up a habit just like that. You will need to focus on *replacing* these behaviors which stem from fearing your personal power. You will need to initiate behaviors that are life-giving, and self-nurturing. You may have to make yourself Number One for a while in order to change, even if you feel guilty about it. You owe it to yourself and everyone around you, to learn it.

It is imperative to *do* something positive to change. You have three choices all the time in every situation. You can:

A.   Accept it as it is

B.   Change it—ACT

C.   Stagnate and doing nothing/build a storehouse of stress = Self-punishment

Whenever you choose C. (to stagnate), you are punishing yourself. Do you know why? This is important to uncover. I have found that anytime we hold ourselves back from positive change or peaceful acceptance, we are avoiding our *fears of personal power*. These fears can even fool us. We can be practicing C.—believing that we are doing A.—hoping for B. to happen. Things do not *just happen*. Action is the only way out and action requires facing your personal power.

Each of the above behaviors is related in some way to the subconscious fear of the perceived result of personal power. Negative emotions such as anger, grief, judgement, denial, distrust, shame and guilt are related to a deep fear of empowerment and knowing who you really are. We suffer also when we feel a lack of control over our feelings.

The Berkeley Wellness Letter comments that "Powerlessness and on the job feelings of being out of control lead to stress and poor performance."

The following fears are part of conditioning. We have learned these behaviors and the emotional states that support them. Each can be uncovered and eliminated from the mind and emotions.

Fears of Personal Power and Presence

Fear of success
Fear of failure
Fear of change
Fear of the unknown
Fear of visibility/being seen
Fear of responsibility
Fear of criticism/being wrong
Fear of rejection/abandonment/being alone.

Much of the confusion is really about our misunderstanding of the true meaning of power. This will be clarified in the chapter on the conditioning of power. If you know what your fears and conditioning are, you can deal with it. Attempting to attack each behavior separately is too long a process and too disconcerting. You will not become more conscious, just more self-conscious. Getting to the root of the fear is important, and when you have discovered it, work on releasing it. This may sound terribly simple, but the most effective way is to acknowledge the fear for its former power over you, and then affirm its release.

Emotional clearing gives you greater ability to empower others.

Managers who understand the unconscious fears of their employees and employees who recognize the fears in their superiors, can more consciously communicate in empowering ways because they can understand and avoid tense interactions. An employee may know a good solution but be afraid to suggest it to the boss. A manager may be aware of a problem, but feel helpless to address it effectively, not due to lack of knowledge, but due to fear of criticism and disapproval.

Employers want honest, accountable, relaxed, motivated, healthy and productive employees. Employees want well-being, security, achievement, challenge, respect and acknowledgement. This can be achieved when the emotional slates are clean.

Stuffing, hiding and denying confuses others. People may perceive what they think is an "insinuation," and that makes them angry. They think, "Did she mean that I am not as good as she?" "Is he angry at me?" or "What did I do wrong?"—and on and on. Pondering an ulterior meaning without clearing it up right away removes you from your true power. The button was pushed, and the tape is rolling. Tapes are constant re-runs that have nothing to do with the person in front of you. There are times when you find yourself saying something that you really want to say to someone else, but the person you're facing is the one who heard it. You may have had a chance to express yourself, yet are not creating positive change. The tapes are your inside conditioning and emotional withholding.

Most of our uncontrollable tapes create stressful interactions. A strained relationship with one's boss or employee is enough to make the job miserable. A tense rapport with family members can keep you in a bad mood for years. Likewise, a negative communication *with yourself* fuels a fire of low self-esteem within, and this flame will eventually burn you. It's called burn-out, and many people suffer from it.

We empower our presence and behave harmoniously with others only when we erase old buttons, clear up the past and strengthen our ability to respond emotionally *in the present*. This requires the process of conscious change.

We are mistaken into thinking that clearing the past is for those who are in therapy. We believe that only those people who are in crisis need assistance in understanding their past and recognizing the need for clearing it up. This is unfortunate. I do not know anyone, nor have I ever met anyone, who is not an eligible candidate for participating in a personal empowerment program which is therapeutic, but certainly not therapy in the traditional context we have socially and intellectually adopted.

There are many people who have graduated beyond the normal therapeutic process of sitting, talking and being listened to, with a few nods and comments here and there to comfort them. These people are ready for some real answers. They are interested in understanding their core issues and how to make new decisions and change *consciously*. This growing number of people knows that they do not need "therapy", but they still have not learned how to take a proactive approach to changing their thoughts, feelings and behaviors. I have spent many years learning how to consciously change through almost exclusively experiential methods. The training I use with clients acts as a bridge between learning and therapy, and has produced measurable results and success for participants beyond my expectations or imagination.

One woman found the mate of her dreams and another was able to let go of a hurtful relationship. The president of a big corporation gained recognition for his highly improved presentation skills; another participant received a promotion, a young woman discovered her life purpose. A real estate agent doubled his income and a beauty consultant increased her sales dramatically.

All participants report a deeper understanding of their lives and a true sense of confidence in knowing how to proceed with life decisions. More and more people have learned the key to conscious change.

Behaviors are a result of emotions. Emotions are a result of state of mind. Change the thought and mental images, and you change feelings and behavior. Sounds simple, but it takes real commitment. Going from self-consciousness to just *consciousness* is the key, which requires a journey into knowing who you really are. You are worth every sacrifice you may make to achieve this knowledge and the reward is precious.

CHAPTER 5

Mental Presence

"The significant problems we have cannot be solved at the same level of thinking we were at when we created them."

Albert Einstein

When you are mentally present, you attain focus and clarity of thinking. Sharp and distinct ideas come to your mind, rather than murky and vague images. The most wonderful part of being present mentally is the inner calm and stillness you experience at will. With training and practice, you can stop mental chatter at any moment and enjoy feeling peaceful and centered.

One time I was late for a business meeting. I had overslept, dressed hurriedly but looked well put together. When I arrived, the meeting had begun and I sat in silence for the duration. My colleagues commented on my lack of participation which they found strange and unusual for me. So did I. I realized that though I was there physically, I never "got there" mentally. I was not mentally present.

In the powerful state of mental presence, you think and act more clearly, because you have greater access to your knowledge. Mental presence is productive in brainstorming sessions, problem solving and all other creative activities. Most of humankind's greatest inventions have been born from a calm state of mental presence.

Mental presence occurs when your mind literally comes to a stop. This means your brain is functioning well, and your thoughts are stilled. Peace of mental silence pervades.

Unfortunately, most people are controlled and run by their thoughts. For instance, when you find yourself driving in your car while replaying in your mind an entire conversation which you had yesterday, then you are out of your mental presence. To spend endless moments in fantasy, reenacting a script you cannot change by telling yourself what you should have said, what you could have done, and what you will do next time, is pure self-talk addiction.

Thinking in sporadic, uncontrollable mind chatter is one of our most disempowering habits. Some people speak with relentless mind chatter, with little awareness that few are really listening. Stopping mental and speech chatter is the greatest gift you can give yourself. It empowers your presence immediately. Without mental presence you cannot be conscious of yourself and those around you. You simply cannot maintain a state of personal presence if your mind is controlling you.

The mind is a function of your self or

"consciousness." It is difficult to study your own consciousness because in the process of observation, it is easy to get lost in the thoughts. Thoughts are a function of the mind, just as the mind is a function of consciousness. The thoughts that run through your mind either raise or lower your awareness. Thoughts have the power to create more openness and perception, or more limitations and denial.

Many of our thoughts result from conditioning. Every individual has a unique subconscious "set-up" filled with dramas and scenarios of the past. The mind has learned to balance this with agreements that have become beliefs. The particular subconscious conditioning of an individual is the very reason why the use of general affirmations does not always work. When the specific set-up for an individual is uncovered, it is possible to design a specific formula that will pierce through that person's unique subconscious thinking habits.

In my training programs these formulas are called the *New Concept of Power and Your Personal Truth*. I wish it were possible to walk you through this in written form, but it is not. It took an experience of your whole self to create these blocks, and it will take an experience of your whole self to unblock them. The technique is not hypnotic and very simple; it has also never failed to work. As a de-hypnotization process, it is natural and safe. The form of questioning applied produces a surprisingly accurate analysis of each person's subconscious beliefs, without having to reveal details of the past. This works wonderfully in a group setting. Within a flash participants have a clear picture of the interconnection of subconscious data which is holding them back. This process allows each participant to uncover her personal blocks to being in her personal power. The limiting thoughts are only lies. Since the limiting thoughts are retrieved *from within* the participant, the process in itself is empowering. The results are the unique formulas that express personal truth—and truth is the most powerful tool we have. You realize that you do know the truth. You just have to go within and search for it.

These modes of thinking have a definite presence about them. Just one thought away and in a few seconds you can be mentally present and empowered or disempowered. It is all your choice.

Modes of Thinking

Empowering	Disempowering
1. Accountability	Blame
2. Letting go of wanting/ needing approval	Wanting/needing approval
3. Letting go of wanting/ needing control	Wanting/needing control
4. Understanding	Judgement
5. Choice thinking	Should Thinking
6. Self-supportive: "More than myself," "my personal best"	Comparison Thinking: "Better or worse than others"

Accountability is the most empowering characteristic of a leader. Accountability is the ability to face the facts and change what needs to be changed.

It's an "Okay, I am 100 percent ready to be accountable for this situation because I know that this attitude is crucial to change and action." Accountability is the opposite of blame—no blame at all, not even blaming yourself. It is easy to admit a mistake, but people have been conditioned to avoid it out of fears of disapproval and criticism. One thought of blame will focus you into the past and denial, and cause you to lose the state in which you have any ability to act.

Wanting approval is an addiction for many people. It is especially prevalent in women who are afraid to act from their power because someone may not like them for it. This is a common trait and it is imperative to overcome this habit in order to be in power and presence. There are no exceptions to this. Those focused on wanting approval are not happy because they are trying to fulfill a need with an outward gesture that can only be satisfied from within.

Wanting approval implies to the mind that you do not have it. Wanting and needing establishes a lack. Then when approval IS there, it is overlooked, deflected or denied. The mind is that powerful.

I was leading a workshop on self-empowerment when a woman expressed her depressed frustration about not getting the job promotion she wanted. The promotion would have required her to work closely with a colleague who was a controlled workaholic and disorganized. When she realized that she wanted that job position only for the sake of approval and not because of its benefits, she was able to let go and not only accept the situation, but was thrilled that she did not get stuck working out her conflicts with the superior in question. She let go of wanting approval which freed her from constant stress. Now she enjoys her work environment.

When you *give up wanting approval*, you immediately experience more of it. Your presence becomes relaxed, centered, confident and sure. You can get on with your work without waiting for constant encouragement. You internalize the support you receive so that you feel sure of who you are and what you are doing. This is apparent in your nonverbal expression. My clients have noticed the difference immediately when they have worked on affirmations for giving up wanting approval. They immediately experienced more recognition.

Wanting Control is a confusion about direction and power. Our perception of power is conditioned by our life experience and this is explained in the next chapter on the *Power of Conditioning*. People resent a controller and avoid telling them the truth because they usually can't handle the truth. The main truth they do not accept is that:

> *It is impossible to really control anyone or anything.*

This is an utter illusion and when the bubble bursts, it is devastating. A controller is disempowered because all the effort of keeping "it" all together is not enough. There is always something more that needs to get "under control." When you think that it is imperative to control everything and everyone, then the task ahead is overwhelmingly hopeless. Controllers get burnt out and run out of ways to motivate others, and finally resort to employing fear and guilt tactics. People resent a controller.

Giving up wanting control is an immense internal relief. Giving up wanting control does not mean that you have given up control. You have only given up WANTING it. When you do that, you feel a wonderful sense of space and time. You can allow yourself to be supported and you are more relaxed, healthy and enjoyable to be around. You open up to learning how to direct the flow of your life, instead of perfecting the control of it. You have the ability to meditate and let go of the past.

Any sentence that begins with *"I should"* or *"They should"* is disempowering. This is an attempt at getting control as well as placing blame. Shoulds do not do anything but create guilt. Guilt is the star of disempowerment and an ineffective presence. Guilt is the poorest motivator. It may bring about action, but with it goes low self-esteem. *Getting rid of your should list is the last should you should ever do.* Replace *I should* with *I would like* and *I choose*. Learn to *feel* what is the right thing to do. Then choose to do it.

Judgement is a hardened form of blame. Where blame is an act of striving to make oneself feel better because of lack of self-esteem, judgement is formed by existing narrow-minded prejudice regarding a situation, a person or group. All prejudice is based on judgement that creates roadblocks to positive communication and problem-solving. Judgement usually has nothing to do with common sense, and is generated out of fear of losing control.

Understanding is comprehension. You have an open mind to new information and are in constant search for a higher viewpoint, no matter what the subject is. Gurdjieff, the great philosopher and teacher said, "Understanding is acquired from the totality of information intentionally learned and from personal experiencing; whereas knowledge is only the automatic remembrance of words in a certain sequence."

Understanding brings referent power, respect, regard, and bonding friendships. With understanding you find purpose in everything and everyone. When you have an understanding mind, your presence is safe and offers security and comfort to others. You can be trusted, because you are truly trust*worthy.*

Comparison thinking is disempowering because you are always "better than" or "worse than" someone else. It propagates continual judgement of others or self-negating feelings. It can foster compulsive behaviors of looking for approval or deflecting achievement.

Supportive thinking empowers you to be your personal best. You support yourself in context of who you are and where you are in your life. This is a common mode of thinking for high performance people. They know how to compete with themselves, to be "more than I was yesterday." They are motivated for greatness, not mediocrity, because it makes them feel good. A supporter can reach wonderful heights and be supportive of others at the same time. A supporter never judges other people or underestimates their abilities, and knows that it is better to see the good in bad people, than the bad in good ones.

Mental Rehearsal

*"Anything the mind can conceive and believe,
it can achieve."*

Jules Verne

Mental rehearsal is the careful programming of positive visions and self-talk into the mind. There are approximately 45,000 to 50,000 thoughts a day that run through your mind, which comes out to about 153 to 300 words a minute. Each and every word that crosses your mind forms a thought that literally affects your mood, action, speech, and even the way that you look.

As we have already discussed, there are empowering and disempowering thought structures that you CHOOSE from everyday. For instance, if someone tells you something demeaning and negative, it will probably affect you. You cannot control what others say to you, but you can control whether you choose to take that thought with you into the future. Every time you agree to maintain a negative thought that you drummed up or that another person has blasted at you, you have the power to accept or reject it. If you have been subjected to a lifetime of negative conditioning, you still *today, right now*, have the choice to hold onto that conditioning as truth, or to reject it as falsehood. You have free will.

An effective method of choosing your beliefs is mental rehearsal. Mental rehearsal comprises the time-honored techniques of affirmations and visualization that have proven to produce success in the lives of many. I know of no one who has been successful in a conscious endeavor who has not learned to master his thoughts, feelings and visions. These are the internal motivators to reaching your potential.

Mental rehearsal is also effective in motivating teams of all kinds—in business, sports and families. The power of mental rehearsal in organizing group thought is profound. An executive tested the idea about group vision. To a group of employees, he gave a puzzle to put together. He told no one what the final picture was supposed to look like. They could not solve the puzzle or put pieces in their place. Then he took one employee at a time into his office, and showed each one a *different* picture of the completed picture. This produced group confusion, tension and frustration. Then he showed them *all at once* what the final picture would look like. He gave them the same *vision*. They put the puzzle together in no time at all.

This exercise represented a form of mental rehearsal. Each employee repeated the vision in his mind, and only had to work at matching the inner picture that was already *in his memory*.

Mental Rehearsal Creates Memory

What we say to ourselves with repetition is called an affirmation. You can choose to think about what you want to happen or what you do not want to happen. Whatever you think about, *expands* and you will get more in your life of the things you think about.

Affirmations are purposely chosen and repeated in the present tense. When you affirm a positive statement in the present tense, then one minute later that thought is already in your memory. The key is that *you always do what you remember.*

This is marvelous. You can practice affirming the positive at any time—driving a car, running, working out, cooking dinner, cleaning dishes, taking a shower or bath. Some effective affirmations are listed in Part Two of this book. You can construct them in your own way. There is true power and presence in both the spoken and unspoken word. Words form thoughts, and a group of thoughts form visions which are symbols that have great meaning to your mind.

A wonderful example of focused thinking occured when I was sitting at a stoplight and looked up at a highrise being constructed, surrounded by cranes. In the past, the thought "Oh, how dangerous it is to be working up there" would have crossed my mind. But this time, my eyes fell on a huge banner inscribed with the message, "Think Safe." I found it difficult to think about anything other than safety. I had been given the vision with a positive suggestion. This experience was a marvelous example of using the power of words in daily life.

You can learn new paradigms of thought, unlearn negative programming, and empower your life with visions of success. It not only becomes noticeable in your behavior and speech, but also in your presence. Your visions are apparent to others as soon as they meet you.

Mental Presence and Breath

One of the most interesting discoveries you will make is the relationship between your mind and your breathing patterns—both are interrelated and affect each other immediately. Try this:

Take three deep breaths, inhale fully, and let it all out while relaxing on the exhale. Check yourself. Aren't you already calmer than a moment ago?

If you have the habit of holding your breath at regular intervals, neither inhaling fully, nor completely exhaling, you will have great difficulty achieving mental presence. The adrenal glands get into their fight or flight mode, to which the body responds with an onset of instant tension—looking about with underlying anxiety, ready for anything.

This mental thought and breathing pattern is learned. This condition puts undue stress on your body and your mind, and gives free rein to the existence of unpleasant emotional states. When you are in this mode, you actually are in the grip of a "low-grade" fear.

You can correct this, by simply being mindful of your breathing pattern and learning to improve it. I have seen people who breathe correctly for the first time in years, break down with a sob. It feels so good to let go, and they are so relieved not to experience the byproducts of their shallow, irregular breathing habits. Life can be more pleasurable with every breath you take.

When I discovered the connection between the mind and the breath, I was in Montana, on the Yellowstone River, fly fishing. After standing in the swirls of the rushing river for eight hours a day, day after day for a week, and concentrating on one thing only—placing the fly exactly where I wanted it to land on the shimmering waters, alert and ready to hook that elusive trout, I noticed that I was becoming more and more relaxed.

I had reached a deep level of peace. My breathing was slow, rhythmic and connected. My mind was focused and deeply aware of the present. I witnessed myself for a while and realized that every so often, a thought bubbled to the surface of my mind as if it had traveled from the bottom of the river. The passion that fly fishermen have for their art was instantly revealed to me. Like other devotees of this solitary sport, I was *meditating* on the fly—silently, still void of any thought chatter to break the calm of my very being.

You can meditate on anything. In fact, you do— on things like: Money, business, careers, family worries, not liking yourself, blaming others, past conversations, old hurts, tomorrow's unknowns, etc. This kind of negative focus disempowers you. The relationship between mind and emotion depicted in the folowing dialogue between Tokimune and his Zen teacher, Bukko, expresses a keen message about meditation.

> *Tokimune:* Of all the ills of life, fear is the worst. How can I be free from it?
> *Bukko:* You must shut off the place where it comes from.
> *Tokimune:* Where does fear come from?
> *Bukko:* It comes from Tokimune.
> *Tokimune:* Tokimune hates fear so much. How can you say it comes from Tokimune?
> *Bukko:* Try and see. Abandon Tokimune and come tomorrow: your courage will be as great as the whole world.
> *Tokimune:* How do I abandon Tokimune?
> *Bukko:* You must simply cut off all thinking.
> *Tokimune:* What is the way to cut off all thinking?
> *Bukko:* Plunge yourself into meditation, and wait for the body and mind to become serene.
> *Tokimune:* My duties in the world leave me so little time. What can I do?
> *Bukko:* Going and sitting and staying and lying, whatever you have to do, that itself is the best place of practice and training.
>
> *Grass Of The Way*

True meditation is an act that focuses on all that is right and whole about you. It has nothing to do with religion, and is an excellent way to *train your mind as if it were a muscle.* Just as your body can be trained to instinctively respond to a specific exercise, so the mind can be trained to maintain calm and stillness while achieving focus, concentration and acute awareness.

Meditation is recommended by doctors, health practitioners, psychologists and counselors as an excellent means of self-therapeutic maintenance. Reduced auto insurance rates are available for meditators in Germany, because studies have shown that people who meditate are more aware, focused, less stressed, and therefore are less likely to have an automobile accident.

When you are mentally present with a quiet mind, empowered thinking, and strength of vision, your knowledge and wisdom emerge. You experience peace of mind. Roleplaying drops and you manifest your real self.

This is the self which knows true power. Our ability to discover our true self within is contingent on our conditioning about power.

CHAPTER 6

The Conditioning Of Power

*"Self-knowledge leads to a profound change
in the individual's definition of power."*

Marilyn Ferguson

*"Personal leadership rests on strength of character,
not power of authority."*

Paul J. Meyer

Empowerment is an ability to achieve goals and act with an effective presence through the medium of true power. All our goals, dreams, and desires, plus what they represent to us, are reflective of the concept of power that we embody in our inner core.

Coming into your presence is to claim your power as a person. Power and presence are inseparable. Both of these "states" are interdependent of each other.

Where there is one, the other is apparent.

Every time you are in a state of presence, whether it be the effect from an external or internal catalyst, you will come face to face with your own power. Every time. When this happens you will either claim that power or fear it. A fear of being in your power affects every aspect of your life as well as your relationships. Managers, for instance, have a hard time empowering others, if they have not embraced their own power by learning the skills of presence. To "empower" is to validate others to discover their strengths and then act on that self-knowledge.

Our concepts of personal power are formed from our conditioning. Our beliefs about power, both socially and individually have a great influence on us. Conditioning is the sum total of influences that have shaped our thinking, feeling and behavior. All our mental definitions and perceptions are influenced by the conditioning of our past—from our parents, friends, teachers and family. The memory system of our mind continues to have a strong influence on our thoughts, speech and actions, many of which are unconscious.

For several years now, an abundance of material has emerged on the subject of conditioning and how our beliefs and the conditioning of our minds with thought patterns affect us.

A better understanding of the workings of the mind is responsible for influencing medicine, science, education, business, industry, religion and art. New frameworks of thought in different cultures are merging. Eastern mythologies and psychologies, and western scientific study of the nature of reality are coming together in a new paradigm, more encompassing than ever before.

Through the genius of quantum physics and the ancient science of consciousness, we now have an understanding that *all that we perceive is a symbol of what we call reality, and that reality is what we believe to be true.* In short:

> *All experience in all reality is a state of mind.*

When we realize that everything is a state of mind—our opinions, beliefs and perceptions (our conditioning) can become a conscious decision. This reality allows us choice, change and re-learning. We can unlearn our conditioning and embrace a new way of thinking. Look at what you believe and ask yourself, "Do I *want* to believe this? Is this belief ultimately good for me and others? Does this belief *support* my goals in life?"

Your beliefs can become a conscious choice. You can question all your thoughts about right and wrong, who you are, your feelings, your body, your mind, your job, your morals, good and evil, life and death, relationships, power, money, joy, pain, religion, spirituality, God, justice, eternity and on and on. You will even question your beliefs about power—*your* own personal power.

Without understanding our conditioning about power, exercises in thought adjustment may not get through the mental blocks caused by past and present limiting beliefs.

Personal presence and empowerment are states of mind. It is important that you embrace the highest ideas about yourself while enhancing your presence, otherwise the changes may not last. It is selfish to block your power and presence with limiting negative thoughts about yourself. It is a selfless act to radiate your personal presence through positive thinking.

Memories are also thoughts which are stored in the subconscious, and are keys to shaping your beliefs. Memories, like all your other thoughts are either helping you or harming you, either empowering you or disempowering.

> *"Memory is the screen on which the present is viewed."*
>
> Sato

The screen of memories can be either a stumbling block or a building block. We carry this screen with us throughout our lifetime. It is important to look at your conditioning and decide if the beliefs are empowering or disempowering. We can decide to keep, change, or enhance it. We can even erase a good part of it. It is very important to stop living in the past and to respond in the present. Only in the present moment can your true power and presence emerge. You can choose the way that you think.

A woman with whom I counseled had the underlying belief that she was wrong. It did not matter what she did that was right, good and successful, her core belief "I am wrong," was powerful enough to keep her frozen in fear when she was about to do something new. Unlocking the subconscious belief and revealing her "rightness" has empowered her actions, thinking, feeling *and* image. Others around her have noticed the change.

We carry our views of power in our conscious and subconscious mind. A fundamental exercise is to insure that your perception of power is not based on negative conditioning of the past or false social definitions. Society defines power as a social and economic status, which is achieved through education, successful careers and material wealth. Today this concept of power is challenged. We are yearning to clarify and reevaluate our motivations in a sincere quest for understanding how to empower ourselves and others at the same time.

Gary Zukav in *The Seat Of The Soul* clearly speaks of the dichotomy of external power *(control)* and internal power. He states, "The perception of power as external splinters the psyche of the individual, the community, the nation and the world."

Over and over I have seen the splintering of individuals' ability to act, to be happy, because their subconscious perceptions of power were based on the conditioned memory that "power equals control". When power and control are mixed up in our minds, the confusion spreads out to influence our relationships. People are conditioned to think that power equals "having power over". Individuals are afraid of their own power because they *believe* it is control. Control, whether you are the "controller" or the "controlled," is fraught with negative states such as fear, guilt, wanting approval, denial, shame, blame and judgement; in short, co-dependent behavior.

Many people are afraid of getting what they deserve in life, because to do so would require them to exercise their power to act. The idea of power brings them face to face with their control issues.

The *One Minute Manager* co-authors said, "Empowerment is all about letting go so that others can get going."

You must let go of old definitions of power in order to claim it and empower others. What you think about power will influence your ability to claim and exercise it in your life. If you think in your subconscious mind that power means either control or loss of control, without knowing why, you will hesitate to claim it. If you think that power is bad, angry, manipulative, abusive, and intimidating, you will not be motivated to empowerment.

You could be blocking your power by simply not knowing the limiting thoughts you have about it. Let's clarify the difference between power and control as defined by Webster.

Power

A. Ability to do or act, capable of doing or accomplishing something.
B. Particular capabilities of body or mind.
C. Delegated authority, exercises authority and influence.

To be "powerful" is to be believable by virtue of clear or incisive presentation, to the point, relevant, pertinent. It is to be strong, mighty, potent, influential, convincing, forcible, effective.

To be "powerless" is to be unable to produce an effect, lacking power to act, to be helpless.

<u>Control</u>
A. To exercise restraint or direction over.
B. To hold in check.
C. To test or compare.
D. To eliminate or prevent the flourishing of something undesirable.
E. Regulation, domination or command.
F. The situation of being under the regulation, domination or command of another.

Negative subconscious conditioning embedded in our memory banks is not about true power at all. True power is confused with coercive power, the medium of control.

> *The negative conditioning of coercive power in the subconscious mind blocks personal power and presence.*

Negative conditioning, expressed as thoughts of self effacement, lack of personal influence and a poor estimate of our ability to achieve a goal, is an attitude we have learned. They have been taught to us. We have to unlearn them and substitute positive thoughts of self value.

When we are able to do this, we begin to exercise personal power. Change your conditioned mind about power, and you will more easily change your habits and strengthen your behaviors.

There are other modes of power too, which are introduced below. These four modes of power are defined in context of your *relationship* with others. You can utilize true power or coercive power in each of these contexts. Your intentions make that choice. Daily self-examination is required in order to remain centered in truth and not be fooled by hidden motives based on fears of losing control and disapproval. When we really examine our fears we find that they are based on false premises and do nothing to help us or others. Our relationships pivot around the form of power being used. There is a very distinct difference between true power and coercive power and how they affect your presence and the roles you play in your relationships, as you will discover later.

Modes of Power

Referent Power: A power that involves having personal respect of others for your qualities, accomplishments, and personal attributes. Others may defer or refer to your opinion or guidance based on their respect for you. They give power to you in their minds.

Legitimate Power: Legitimate power resides in an authority relationship. You legitimately have some power over others due to your position in which you are free to make decisions that will affect others.

Expert Power: The power that derives from being an expert in a particular field. You may be sought out for your knowledge in a specific area and have the power to influence a decision based on your specialized knowledge.

Reward Power: Reward power derives from your ability to give psychological and material rewards to others, such as a position or a compliment. This person may be responsible for the resources, say the main breadwinner, or the one who handles the bread may be the one with reward power. A secretary at work may be in the position to get you into a job or keep you out. We all know about "getting past the front desk".

Coercive Power: This type of power is acted out by dismissing, demoting, demeaning, discounting, reducing status, reprimanding or taking away privileges. This can be related to legitimate power—but not always. This form of power is common in disempowering relationships.

True Power is an internal state of being *present* in body, mind and spirit. It is a manifestation of pure presence, that is centered in truth. True power resides within you and exists regardless of your relationships with other people. This is your internal domain, your relationship with yourself alone. Anyone can have it, all have the potential for it, regardless of social and economic position. True power is an internal reservoir of energy that comes from the spiritual self—the Witness—when the body, mind and emotions are cooperating as a team. This is further discussed in Chapter Eight.

When mental, emotional and physical self are not working as a team due to blocked unconscious energy and inhibitions, the spiritual self is veiled, perhaps even hidden or denied in life experiences.

When the three selves of *personality*—physical, mental and emotional—are not in a state of presence, then our thoughts, emotions and behaviors form *roles*. We agree to play disempowering roles because some aspect of ourselves has been projecting from our past conditioning of fears. Even our appearance is part of the role-playing game.

Role-playing is the outer manifestation of communication patterns in relationships. These communications are verbal as well as non-verbal. Role-playing occurs when you are not present, and the *Real You* within, the Witness, is veiled. The Witness is a state of true presence that is beyond role-playing. But before we get into that, let's look at the false roles people play.

CHAPTER 7

Role Playing

"We don't see things as they are, we see them as we are."

Anaïs Nin

"Actions speak louder than words."

Shakespeare discerned that we are all players on the stage of life. Everyone else is our audience, whether they be conversing with us in our kitchen, watching us at work, or listening to our presentation. Our audiences include our children, mates, co-workers, bosses, clients, neighbors and friends. There is someone watching us most of the time.

We have neatly divided the stage on which we perform into two parts: The front stage and back stage. We seek to perform at our best on the front stage, and try to keep backstage material hidden from our audiences.

There is a problem when this backstage agenda reaches the front stage. Perhaps a company's disregard for hiring minorities makes newspaper headlines; a husband finds out his wife is having an affair; the politician's secret makes it to the evening news.

There are times when the backstage is in the limelight and only too visible. Therefore, it is vital to have our values, principles and character in alignment with our outer projected image. Our backstage behavior is as equally important to personal presence as the front stage. Behavior that one would not want someone outside of the immediate family to see, is not a desirable trait or habit to maintain.

Bridging the gap between the front and back stage behavior is imperative to personal presence. You actually have to be convinced of your authenticity. It is important that you really *be* the person you project to be.

> *Who You Really Are,*
> *Who You Project To Be,*
> *Who You Want To Be, and*
> *Who You Think You Are*
> *Can all be synchronized together as a whole self.*

When this happens, you are beyond playing a role, you easily create interdependent relationships, you are self-empowered. You are carrying the power of personal presence. You are, simply put, being yourself—true self, the Witness which is not a role at all. Socrates summed it up when he said, "Be that which you wish to seem."

When synchronization of self does not happen, role playing appears. Role playing limits our field of expression and inhibits our ability to act effectively.

Role playing creates disempowerment, co-dependent interactions, limiting modes of thinking and unwanted feelings. Role playing blocks intimacy, productivity, creativity and communication.

Role playing is determined by the degree that we agree to be "set up" as a specific kind of person who will interact in a predictable, expected way. When others bind us to roles that we agree to fulfill, there is little room for change and growth. We can be labeled based on how we look, speak, think and behave.

Most of all, role playing blocks personal presence, and lack of personal presence propagates role playing. This produces a bonafide merry-go-round. Everyone wants to "get off," but people are often totally unaware of the roles so they sense that something is wrong, but can't pinpoint the problem.

Some of the characteristics of each role are actual qualities which we can acknowledge in ourselves and admire in others. As you read, remember that there is a difference between *caring* which is empowering and playing the *mother* role which is disempowering. To be *motivating* is an excellent quality, but to be positioned as a *cheerleader* without getting into the game is frustrating and ultimately defeating; *winning* is the mark of an achiever, but to personally *play to win at all costs* is a detriment to oneself and other team members.

When our qualities become a role that is expected, we are limited in our ability to just be ourselves. We are always changing and need to encourage each other to consciously grow and change, instead of disempowering each other with roles which inhibit creative expression.

Our image and our behavior are interconnected within the boundaries of roles we play. Standards of beauty and image actually express behaviors.

Gloria Steinem says in *Revolution From Within,* that *"Beauty is less about looks than about behavior ... Once we get a grip on an understanding that, for males or females, standards of beauty (image) are really about what society wants us to do or not to do, then we can affect them (standards) by taking power into our own hands and altering the way we behave... behind the form of what is considered beautiful, there is always the function of what is considered acceptable to do. Thus, before we accept a standard of beauty (or image) for ourselves, we can ask, do I really like the behavior it symbolizes?"*

Roles

Men	Women
Father/Protector	Mother/Nurturer
Little Boy	Little Girl
Winner	Cheerleader
Superman	Superwoman
Playboy	Seductress
Iron Man	Iron Maiden

1. Role: *Mother*
   People (both men and women), seek her out to tell her their problems. She is set up to be a

nurturing, never-critical mother image. No one wants her to be frank, direct, and action-oriented, since she is set up to be the care-taker.

Results: She is expected to be available at any hour to take care of the latest emotional/mental upheaval. Her goals are limited to nurturing others to reach their goals, while losing sight of her own. She loses her effectiveness in decision making, critical discernment and demonstration of her competence. Others will not want her to give action-oriented suggestions. She will not be taken seriously. She may feel that she has to get angry to be heard, which surprises everyone but does not change the role. People just think she is having a bad day.

If this is true for you—reflect on the following questions:
• With whom have you been playing this role and are you still playing it?
• How does this affect your ego?
• Do you need to be needed?
• Do you really believe if men or women ask for your emotional support that you are demonstrating your work skills?
• Are you afraid of your power as a woman?
• Do you fear that you will be left alone if your claim your power?

Action: Stop letting yourself be set up. Remember YOU created this role and you can change it. You are giving your power away. Recognize your need for approval and give up *wanting it.* Only then can your personal power emerge. If you are that good at the mother role, charge for your counseling services.

2. Role: *Seductress*
    She is desirable to converse with over lunch, coffee, etc. Men want to *support* her. She is an expert in getting men to listen to her problems (her past traumas, family problems, etc.) Men vie to position themselves to be her number one protector. The boss (male) will probably win out. She is viewed as overly flirtatious, but she is unconscious of these impressions herself. Men either want to protect, avoid, or conquer her.

    Result: Resentment from other males toward her protector, and their special relationship (even without any sexual involvement). Jealousy from other females appears because she has received more attention, and they have watched the males volley for her (even though they would never admit their competitive games). She may get the promotion due to the fact that her protectors may be more aware of her skills. She becomes a source of tension, resentment and jealousy, as her peers try to hide their true (embarrassing, but unable to be fully stuffed) feelings. In this case, her professional actions will often be thwarted. If she is productive, the credit will go to her protector. If in fact, she does have a sexual relationship with her protector, she will have lost all respect from her co-workers, and when the man has had enough of her or she threatens him in any way, he will terminate the relationship and probably eliminate her position.

If this is true for you—reflect on the following questions:

- With whom have you been playing this role?
- Why do you feel that you need approval for your femininity from males in order to achieve your goals?
- How does this stroke your ego?
- Are you doing this out of a desire to control or need for approval?
- Do you think that your worth is partly determined by your sexual attractiveness to men?
- Do you feel approved of, and more in control, when men desire you?
- Do you use unconscious sexual undertones in your voice, body language and/or clothing. Do you use "bedroom eyes?" (Ask a friend to be honest with you on this one. Any teenager could tell you also.)

<u>Action:</u> Stop letting anyone, especially a male, protect you from a perceived defeat, fall, truth, criticism, etc. You may have to tell him that you

don't need or want his protection. He, in turn, is out of his own power by fearing to let you exercise your own. Watch the amount of attention you allow males to give you concerning your personal problems. Fulfill your need for "fatherly concern" from someone outside of your work environment. As you come to act fully from your personal power, you find that you will not need it. Make a point to heal possible sexual issues and the need for approval from others. You are worthy just by your own appraisal. Men—no one for that matter—can give you what you will not give yourself. Watch your body language, your attire and tone of voice. This can be done without diminishing your femininity and attractiveness. You will simply be powerful and attractive at the same time, rather than seductive. Save it for the real thing.

3. Role: *The Cheerleader*

   She is cute, fun to have around—a true cheerleader type. She supports and encourages her peers enthusiastically as they tackle the really important problems. She watches admiringly from the sidelines wondering when they are going to let her into the game. She is the perpetual positive strokes person who is waiting for permission to take action.

   Results: When the cheerleader attempts to enter the game and speak out, others will try to put her in her place. Isn't she cute? Wasn't that a bright idea? (as if this is unusual for her). She is complimented on *how* she said something, not *what* she said. The reactions of others may cause her to respond girlishly, ever seeking more approval as a member of the group. She is simply happy just to be included. Among female peers, she may be more accepted for her cuteness, because she is non-threatening— neither motherly/*smotherly* or sexually competitive. However, her female peers will not respect her lack of power either.

If this is true for you—reflect on the following questions:
- With whom do you play this role?
- Are you overly complimentary to a male who is doing a routine job?
- Are you playing up to his ego, in order to get approval and control yourself?
- Are you afraid to get tackled, and therefore, feel safer on the sidelines?
- Do you think you will move up, gain respect or be able to demonstrate your competence "by being cute"?
- Are you seeking acceptance as part of the crowd?

Action: Grow up. Be assertive about what you mean. Never talk about your being short or petite, or mention how big men seem to you. Tall women, large women and strong women are not depicted as "cute." Think BIG. Stop complimenting men on every little thing they do. Lower your tone of voice. If you really are small and cute-looking, you need to be extra conscious of your clothing. Translate cute to chic. Use your energy to look taller. Gain the courage to be criticized. Dare to succeed. Walk in your power.

4. Role: *Little Girl*
    She is sweet, feminine and cute. Everybody thinks of her as such a *nice* person. She looks up to powerful men as father figures whose ideals and responsible attitudes include concern for her well-being. She is non-threatening because she has no power. She is obsessed with doing the right thing, getting permission before she takes action and wants approval. She wants to be taken care of in a group and shuns acknowledging her leadership skills.

    Result: She has the uncanny ability to get others to help her with the most mundane jobs—especially men will come to her aid. Women do not feel threatened by her in any way, but she has low credibility among her peers. Few listen to her at meetings but everyone is very nice not to hurt her feelings. People act surprised at her age, but for the wrong reason—not only because she may look young for her age, but because her whole presence is immature.

If this is true for you—reflect on the following questions:

- Are you afraid to speak up?
- Do you think people will disapprove if you give solid constructive criticism?
- Would you rather give advice to others and let them take the heat if it is wrong, but also the acknowledgement if it is right?
- Do you really just want someone to take care of you?
- Do you ask everyone else what you should do about almost everything in your personal life and work?
- Do others tell you that you are naive?
- Do you think that there are "men's jobs" and "women's jobs?"
- Do you catch yourself speaking with a child's tone of voice, or tilting your head when you are listening?

<u>Action:</u> Mature. Heal your inner child. Stop relying on others to lead you. Take some action to be decisive about something, anything. This will develop your confidence in decision making. Avoid telling everyone at work all the details of what is going on in your life—just get on with it. The best solutions are in your own head. Don't waste energy by trying to feel better or getting approval and sympathy from others. ACT.

Learn to say no. Become aware of your strengths and what you are indeed doing well.

Acknowledge yourself for it.

Empower your body language by holding your head straight, lowering your tone of voice, and looking people straight in the eye.

5.   Role: *Superwoman*
She has to do everything herself, because she believes that she is the best person to do the job. A perfectionist in all her roles in life, at work, social hostess, wife, mother. She is never satisfied with her completed work, always striving to do better. She does what she thinks she "should" instead of feeling what is right. She has incredibly lengthy lists to do, do, do. She says "I should," instead of "I choose" which makes her a victim of a life that is running her.

Result: She does not have enough time or inner resources to take care of herself—literally—her physical, mental, emotional and spiritual health. She does four jobs in the time others do one, or so it appears. She does not accept support from others, because she is the perfect caretaker (mother role), cheerleader (pet role), male attention-getter (seductress role). She is depleted of her power. She is driven to perfection, nothing is ever good enough for her vision. She does not give herself acknowledgement and approval, and therefore, strives for it all day long. She is most likely "married to the company." She has difficulty delegating.

She is the die-hard workaholic. She is exhausted. Burn out looms ahead.

If this is true for you—reflect on the following questions:
- In which ways do you play this role?
- Do you really think that you can do everything better than anyone else?
- When was the last time that you enjoyed life?
- Do you think that you are complete?
- Do you have to be in the middle of all office affairs?
- Are you the first one asked to take on another project?
- Have you considered that you are asked to do more because you will not say "No", instead of being the best person for the job?
- Do you go to many social meetings dressed in your business attire?
- Are there key areas in your life that are imbalanced?

<u>Action:</u> Stop, at least slow down. Chill out, or you are going to suffer even more. You are in a situation where you must take accountability for the life that is ruling you. Stop pretending that you must accomplish everything on your list before you will be happy. Be careful that you do not put your healing on list of things to do either. Erase the "should" list and make choices in your life. Figure out what is making you run

from your inner self, and why you are so afraid of your feelings. You probably need a health check-up, a vacation and a heart-to-heart with the person you love. Since you have not taken care of your own needs for so long, develop a self-nurturing plan of action, and then commit to implementing it. Discover your life purpose and use it to gauge all your activities and priorities.

6. Role: *The Iron Maiden*

She is neither motherly, sexually responsive, nor cute. She commands respect to the point that others are not sure of her role—so they put her in the "bitch" persona. She gets tagged with this unflattering label because she has successfully circumvented attempts to be placed in one of the above four roles. Within a few minutes of conversing, she can detect when someone is trying to place her in a role. She has perfected the ability to say "NO" with no guilt. She has let go of the need for approval, though she still seeks some control. Approval doesn't phase her and she cannot be patronized. She is direct—too direct sometimes. She demands equal treatment, respect and power, for the person she *is,* not for the position she holds.

She is in her power, but has not yet "settled" into a fully *harmonious application* of it. She has not yet learned to weigh her intuition, approach life from her heart and empower others with her strength, vision, and focused direction.

Result: People are not always going to like her, but almost everyone will respect her. She may be called cold (because she won't play the nurturing mother) and a man-hater (because she doesn't respond coyly to male sexual innuendos). She may be distrusted (because she is not a cute cheerleader). People are not sure how to handle her. Some avoid interacting with her because they may get a very direct, frank common sense response. On the up side, she is rarely interrupted in her work—no one would dare.

People do not like to have their dirt kicked up before them, which the iron maiden is competent at doing. If she were male, he would be admired for his impeccable insight and irreproachable integrity. As a woman she will be called tough and insensitive because she will not play the mother, daughter or seductress. This can throw some men off and they respect her but are happier going home to their mother/cheerleaders. Though she acts with self-actualization, she is often perceived as aloof and distant.

If this is true for you—reflect on the following questions:
- Do you ever feel like you intimidate others? Do you?
- Do you feel misunderstood?

- Do you ever wonder if you "should" hold yourself back and then shrug it off and decide not to, knowing that is too easy?
- Do other women feel jealous of you?
- Do you need to make a conscious effort not to enlighten someone?
- Do men want to conquer you, or taunt you by sneering at "women's issues?"
- When you are feeling tired and frustrated, do you get too judgmental?
- Do you feel like you are pioneering new courses?
- Do you sometimes feel lonely and wish to find kindred spirits?

Action: You are intelligent. Develop your self-worth to equal your creative ideas. This action eliminates the aloofness that you project. Do not let others make you feel bad, or out of place because of your power. Go for it. Stay in your power and make a conscious effort to assist women around you to exercise their own power. Develop sincere caring and concern. Eliminate arrogant thinking—especially cynical, sarcastic comments and tone of voice. Consciously be supportive instead of judgmental. Seek out other women like you. Develop male friends who treat you as an equal.

Always watch the boundaries of the relationship, so that you do not get tempted into playing the other three roles during a moment of insecurity. Continue to evaluate yourself more than you do others. Let others shine in your presence. Do not hold back your gifts, power, beauty, visions or actions in order to make others like you more. They won't appreciate your effort. Find people who understand you.

Soften around the edges; learn to be gentle with your tone of voice. Be kind. Teach what you know and maintain high expectations of others while supporting them to reach their goals. Seek to understand more than to be understood. Be forgiving. Trust and let go. Lead with your heart.

Men

1. Role: *Father*
   He sets himself up to be the provider. He works very hard to provide for the family which he creates in his work as well as home life. He readily dispenses fatherly advice to others and guards and protects his flock. He projects the flawless boy scout image. Everyone looks up to him for solutions to every problem. A sense of security surrounds him, whether he is secure in himself or not.

   Result: He plays this role at the expense of his health. At the office, he may take care of the women and intervene for them in what HE thinks is a situation too tough for a woman. His role unfolds at the expense of emotional balance in his relationships. This role is disempowering because when he is too busy providing for everyone else his spiritual and emotional selves are inhibited. He does not empower women to perform at their intellectual potential—because wherever there is the father, there is the little girl. He protects women from information that may worry them, which limits the resources of their power to assist him. This leads him to make poor decisions, which is difficult for him to face. If he has a financial setback he feels like a failure. He has difficulties being intimate and showing his true feelings.

If this is true for you—reflect on the following questions:
- Do you often withhold information from women in order to protect them or not worry them?
- Do you listen to women and feel concerned for them, but fail to give them sound directions in the way you would a fellow male? Or do you simply listen and console them?
- Are you uncomfortable expressing your true feelings to others?
- Do you feel a burden of responsibility?
- Do women at your work and in your social life look up to you for advice all the time?

Do they frequently ask your permission
about their actions?
• Does it stroke your ego to have others
looking up to you for advice on a daily
basis?
• Are you sought out on social occasions to
be a listener to the latest female drama?

Action: Let the women around you grow up.
Stop being an emotional caretaker. Refuse to
see the women around you as helpless girls who
need a man. Do not refer to women as girls or
gals. Befriend empowered women who will be
honest with you and let you drop your role.
Stop withholding information from others—that
will be the true support which forces them to
respond in their own ways to situations—even
if it may be uncomfortable for them at first.
This act empowers them and makes you
happier. Recognize that your withholding is not
protecting the other person, but is a hidden
agenda of control.

2. Role: *Little Boy*
   He is the pleaser, the do-gooder who spends a
   lot of energy collecting brownie points for the
   future. He is detail-oriented and willing to do
   minor jobs. He is friendly with strong women
   and prefers to communicate with them. He
   seeks strong women with the power to reward
   and is motivated to patronize them. The little
   boy tries to please everyone around and looks

for approval from his co-workers and boss.

Result: He is quite efficient but rarely taken seriously by his peers. He runs around doing minor tasks even if he has legitimate authority. Women control him. He often feels shamed or emasculated because he does not feel appreciated or approved.

If this is true for you—reflect on the following questions:
- Are you concerned about how your manager "feels" when he/she walks into the office for the day?
- Do you watch for signs of your supervisor's state of mind, and if you can't tell, go into her office to feel out the situation?
- Do you rush back and share your assessment with others?
- Are you a funny person to have around, but when it comes to serious issues you don't contribute anything?
- Do you whine? Are you afraid of losing your job?
- Do you find it hard to take criticism?
- Do you "justify" people's comments about you?
- Do you enjoy gossip?
- Do you play up to the person who has reward power in your office?
- Do you often feel insecure and uncertain?

Action: Grow up. Heal. Stop looking for someone to lean on. Acknowledge your own competence and act accordingly. Stop letting other people control you with their attitudes. Give up wanting approval and control. Be smart and use your energy to build up true character and inner equity. Stop amassing brownie points and patronizing others. Be honest and sincere. Approve of yourself. Start forming your own opinions. Stand your ground for things you believe in. Develop your character and courage.

3. Role: *Superman*

   He is the one in control of every decision going on around him. He knows everything, does everything himself and oversees the minutest details of every operation. He will play any role required in order to get the job done. He is competent, but unable to share his responsibilities. He does not believe that a job can get done without him. He likes to be the savior of people and circumstances. He looks for damsels in distress.

   Result: He is the classic workaholic who misses what is going on around him emotionally. Just as the superwoman falls into the trap of super-doing at work and at home, the superman constantly super-thinks—he can't get business off his mind. Even at home he is consumed with business. He has difficulty calming his mind chatter even while reading a novel on vacation—if he takes one. He cannot sleep because there is just too much to do. His co-workers do not feel that he trusts and appreciates their abilities. He does not believe that others can get the job done without him. They have to report to him for the most miniscule details. Since he cannot delegate properly, he ends up making serious long-range mistakes by focusing too much on the details. He is tired, health issues are appearing while he just plows deeper into the work to avoid facing his feelings.

If this is true for you—reflect on the following questions:

- Do you think your way is the best and only way?
- Can you let a colleague handle a job without checking in on him every five minutes?
- Are you afraid to let go?
- Do you secretly fear that if you are not productive all the time, you will not be needed at all?
- Are you working for love?
- When you are asked how you feel, are you confused about what that means?

Action: Slow down and enjoy life more. Stop and smell the roses. Your friends and family will give a sigh of relief when you change your pace. Pay attention to the feelings of those around you, and you may get in touch with your own feelings. Take a deep rest and learn to just BE. Meditate and read a good book just for yourself. Stop putting off taking care of your health until the next Century. You want to be around to see it. Learn ways you can be as productive with less work hours. Work smarter, not harder.

4. Role: *Winner*

   He is the ultimate super achiever who must play every game and win. He requires a great deal of emotional support and encouragement to stay in the game and play relentlessly. He is highly competitive—to the point that he is anxious about it. He spends hours dreaming up ways to manipulate others and he calls this strategy. He does not like to lose, and is not always a good team player. He fears that others are trying to control him. He will not accept being anything less than Number One. He may talk about being a team player but in the end he sabotages his teammates in order to score a personal triumph. He will play any of the above roles for the purpose of winning at all costs.

   Result: He is simply not happy. He is insecure and has to prove his worth with constant wins. He can easily rally support and motivation from others, yet eventually they learn to disrespect his all-or-nothing win attitude and his inability to be a good loser. Since he has to be the best, he is uncomfortable with others who are his

equal. People do not feel that he looks after
their interests and feel used. He is lonely, but is
more comfortable as a loner. He ponders why
some people will not get too close to him as a
friend.

People don't trust him when they discover
what really motivates him—his own points. He
may be the star player, but in the long run he
will lose if he does not let go of his ego and
work for, not against, the team.

*If this is true for you—reflect on the following
questions:*

- Do you want to be right or do you want to
  be happy?
- What is really the important part about
  winning?
- Do you think others are there to serve you?
- How many people do you have true respect
  for?
- Are you afraid of letting go and losing
  control?
- Do you think that it is stupid to trust others?
- Do you call people "saps" when they are
  gullible?
- Do you really like yourself, or are you just
  pretending in order to win?
- Do you enjoy intimidating others?
- Do you fear empowering others around
  you?

Action: Heal your fears of losing control. Stop

abusing and intimidating others with speech, thought and action. Change your attitudes or you will end up alone. Open your heart in order to connect with others in a new, rewarding way. Learn to value every human and see their good. Empower those who support you instead of using them to your advantage. Open your heart and learn to be a true leader. Care.

The "Winner" role has been adopted by some women who have been Iron Maidens for some time, which results in having to face a choice. They can grow out of role playing and get in touch with their Witness, or find male role models such as the Winner. This is an unfortunate turn for women. When this happens, they stop being concerned for the welfare of men and challenges of other women in business, because they are in it solely for themselves. There are better ways to break the glass ceiling.

5. Role: _Iron Man_
   He is bold, tough, courageous and has great endurance. He can withstand both physical and emotional pain, and that makes him good at making hard decisions when dealing with people. He prides himself on controlling his feelings and his power of reasoning. He is the one you can count on the most to be there to hold the fort. He is powerful, but is still not opened to his full heart-mind connection and true power. He has everything except

acceptance and emotional vulnerability.

Result: He is a tough and dominating man who at no cost ever admits what he is feeling. He is the macho man. He plays the game well and is perceptive, but when it comes to letting go, being vulnerable and taking an emotional risk, he can't cut it. Women may find him insensitive and impossible to deal with—especially on issues where he denies his feelings. Human relations are his downfall. Underneath he feels that women are there to serve him, and he tends to become annoyed when confronted on the issue. Denial is his biggest challenge which of course he denies vigorously.

He angers others easily and pretends that nothing is wrong. He does not consider how others feel, which earns him a degree in insensitivity. He misses the finer qualities in the people around him. Though the old boy's network is crumbling, he secretly still believes in it, which makes others think he is chauvinist and backward in his thinking. He is quite opinionated.

If this is true for you—reflect on the following questions:
- Do you secretly wish for the days when women's and men's roles were simply defined?
- Do you want to have a wife who takes care of you and stays at home (not only for the

children, but for you)?
- Would you be comfortable with a woman as a boss?
- Do you believe that if you show your emotions, it denotes weakness?
- Do you pride yourself in being able to handle other people's grief without shedding a tear yourself?
- Do you believe that all men would benefit from military training?
- Do you think that women are overly emotional?

Action: Learn to let down your guard and be more sensitive. Let your real self emerge and let your feelings show. You will find that people will respect you for your courage. Discontinue playing tired, old male macho roles that will leave you feeling empty and sometimes hopeless—if only you could admit that even to yourself. Let the women around you claim their power by acknowledging them. Avoid doing that job for them. Stop trying to control them. Learn to admit when you are wrong without thinking that you will appear weak. Regard your feelings as a strength rather than a depleter of energy. Support others to grow. Learn to cry.

6. Role: *Playboy*
He is a brash, flirtatious and charming easy talker. He can get the job done but has to converse with everyone in the office about it.

He likes to know everyone—especially the women, their body size, and what they are wearing that day. He thinks of himself as the woman's dream catch, and is noticeably surprised when they ignore him—which they do often.

Result: He is a real damper for women and men just put up with him. Women often feel exposed and vulnerable around him as if he can see through their clothes. If they are not empowered, they will feel intimidated and lose their strength in speech and action. If they are empowered, they have to resort to the iron maiden role. He wastes a lot of his own and other people's precious energy and work time being in a cheeky mood around the office. He is not taken seriously and appears to be irresponsible and untrustworthy.

If this is true for you—reflect on the following questions:
•   Do you really think that flirting at work and embarrassing women is something that they like?
•   When a women does not know how to respond verbally to you, do you think that you have flustered her into being attracted to you?
•   Do you know that other men laugh behind your back?
•   If you dropped your facade and were real

with others, do you think that you would go completely unnoticed?

- Do you use body language that invades other people's boundaries, perhaps without realizing it? Do others back up when you talk to them?
- Do you think your rhetoric is entertaining?
- Have you noticed that mostly young and naive people take you seriously?
- Has anyone ever insinuated your name and reputation in the same breath as sexual harassment?

Action: Get to work. Stop bugging others for you own entertainment. Let go of needing a thrilling escape from feeling so bored with life. Look honestly in the mirror and begin to see something deeper than your surface. Focus your energy on being productive and motivating others in a positive safe way. Learn to listen. Be willing to give up the center of attention at meetings. Let go and be your real self and others are able to do that with you. Dare to be real. Give up wanting approval and control.

• • •

People are likely to play several of these roles in their lives. Different people can bring out different characteristics in us. When one person is glued to a role and will not evolve beyond it, others have difficulty communicating with him/her clearly. The roleplayer perceives the communication *in context of the role being played in the relationship* and not the real person. All of these roles require a state of *"mis-*presence"—a state when one is mentally, emotionally and physically not present. When roles such as these are played, the past is reenacted again in the present. You set one person up as a father image, another as your cheerleader and another as your child.

Often, when people want to drop a role, others around show obvious signs of discomfort. They say: "Who does she think she is?" "Why doesn't he want to listen to me whine anymore?" "When are they going to tell me what's really going on?"

Carl Jung studied families in which one member's behavior seemed to play a role that affected the rest of the family, ie: the alcoholic, the black sheep, the problem child—one person whose behaviors can be changed and around which the whole family becomes focused, to the point of being *generated* by the problem and disturbing behavior. Jung observed that the very family members who adamantly wanted the "problem member" to change and who had invested much energy toward this objective of change, actually *subconsciously* worked to keep him stuck in that role. When the problem member achieved a positive change, Jung found that the other family members resisted the inevitable change of roles which ensued among the group. That resistance often resulted in the other members subconsciously putting the changed member back into the problem role.

Changing a role can rock the boat, but remaining in a role you no longer want, chips away at your self-esteem until it's all whittled away. When you play a role, others *think* they understand you, but you feel this void within, because if you don't understand yourself, then how can they?

The roles that we have played in our family of origin are often the same roles we set up around us in our work environment. These roles can be disconcerting and create stress because we believed we had left those roles behind. Sometimes just by the way that we look, others try to plug us into a role. For instance, if we are overweight, we may be seen as mothers; if we are chic and successful we are pigeoned-holed as iron maidens; if we are petite males we are perceived as little boys; if we are quiet, shy and masculine we are set up as iron men. It is annoying to be put in our place, without being consulted first, a decision based purely on perception.

Take care that your attire, speech, actions or thoughts are not limited to a role which will make it difficult for you to break out of the box others have put you in, or which you have readily agreed to occupy.

The best alternative is to evolve beyond role playing and become authentic. The authentic self becomes the focus, while little attention is given to perceived inventions and *mis*-presentations. There is an insufficient number of role-models which go beyond role playing, but the numbers are growing. Conscious change is a vital characteristic for them. Personal presence is inevitable as a natural instinct.

CHAPTER 8

Spiritual Presence: The Witness

"Know thyself."

Socrates

*And Jesus said to them: When you make the two one,
and when you make the inner as the outer,
and the outer as the inner, and the above as the below,
and when you make the male and female into a single one—
then you shall enter the kingdom."*

St. Thomas

"No one can fail who seeks to reach the truth."

A Course in Miracles.

The Witness is the true self, the *spiritual presence,* which resides within. The Witness observes the world from an objective viewpoint, a more transcendent state and has a wider view of your life and the world.

Your real self is beyond role playing, beyond disempowering communications, beyond wanting control and approval, beyond keeping up appearances. It does not blame, judge, fear or fight. The Witness does not think negatively, hold onto self-limiting thoughts, store past conditioning or degrade the body. The Witness is not what you appear to be, but who you really are.

It is an internal spiritual guide who communicates with you whenever your body, mind and emotions are receptive and in a state of presence. The Witness has a very definite voice within.

The main function of the Witness is to contact the other three selves to develop and maintain clear communication with them. When you have an awareness of mental and emotional presence, when you are in the NOW, a space opens and the spiritual self comes through loud and clear. Communication from the Witness is experienced by a sense of well-being in the body, hearing an inner voice through the mind, and feeling emotions of great intensity which are joyful and comforting.

Another function of the Witness is to help you clear up the past, teach you to love yourself and others, and give you a vision of your self-worth. Once your self-worth and self-esteem are established, the Witness reveals your life purpose.

Unless you become mindful of the Witness, you cannot maintain a state of presence, be self-empowered, sense your self-worth or empower other people. The Witness is concerned with your safety and taking care of your body and mind, because that is the home in which it lives. Anything you do to improve your skills and attitudes, your attributes and abilities are happy events for the Witness. The more you accept conscious growth within yourself, the more you will have access to the voice of your Witness.

The Witness reveals to you keen insights, original solutions and a rush of creative thoughts. This is known as intuition, which I have found makes plain common sense most of the time. There are no coincidences or accidents in the world of the Witness. Everything has an order and everything has a purpose.

The Witness is the source of your true power of personal presence. You can gain respect, trust and loyalty from people because you can be trusted. You approach all your relationships at work with sincerity and from the heart. You are respected in both male and female arenas that are interdependent and synergistic, because there is no question of your birthright, purpose and direction. Some people do not regard you as either man or woman, because the Witness is androgynous. You achieve recognition for who you are, not based on your gender but for your qualities and character. People deal with the real you.

This spiritual connection gives us our measure of happiness and we are perceived as trustworthy and honest—simply because we are. There is no denial lurking in the depth of this spiritual self. In fact, the face of truth always has a positive effect in our professional and personal lives. Truth is always healing, transforming, and empowering.

When you connect with your Witness, it will empower you on all levels and revitalize your image from the inner to the outer. However, in order to do this, several layers of misconceptions and negative beliefs may have to be eliminated.

When the emotions are repressed, and the mind is chattering, the Witness remains vague and muffled in the background. If you want to empower yourself and others—at work or at home—lifting the veils of false beliefs, clearing up your past and claiming the truth is the key. This naturally leads to the connection of your Witness, which is an experience difficult to describe. If you are not sure that you have experienced your spiritual self, then you can be certain that you haven't done so. You will know it when it happens.

> *"One instant is eternity;*
> *Eternity is now.*
> *When you see through this one instant,*
> *You see through the one who sees."*
>
> Wu-Men

Witness gives you a sense of self that surpasses mental understanding.

> *To Know Witness Is To Experience Direct*
> *Perception Of Truth.*

Your Witness is the source of all your inner visions and wisdom. Though you may "know" things, you will not always understand how you know them. You will sense and perceive information about other people that you may not wish to know. With spiritual presence, you may even be misunderstood. Others may wonder, "What is it about you, anyway?" They may wonder *how* you know the things you know. Well, how does a child read the adults around him? How does a dog know when you are afraid? How does the oak tree know how to grow from the acorn?

This is the mystery of life, which is what makes it so wonderful. Knowing that you can go within to learn from this wise inner source, one that loves and cares for you, is a great thing. So many of us have not discovered it. We are very distracted with the outer world of form and image, which is constantly changing. But we can go within and experience the internal constant from which our true presence flows. We can identify with our true identity. We can turn our attention away for a minute and look within. To do this we need methods of bringing our mind, body and emotions to a state of presence. The whole purpose of the other three selves is to come to the still point, in the *now*, in form, thought, feeling and action; then we access our authentic presence.

There is no human being who is exempt from this potential. No one is more worthy of it than another.

You can say that you have a Witness, but this is incorrect. You are the Witness, and you have a body, mind and emotions. You have a *personality,* your body, mind and feelings which are descriptions of you—but they are not you. You are the Witness, the *impersonality* which is eternal. Your personality can be shaped and molded to better reflect your true impersonal self. When you repeat affirmations of self-empowerment, you can believe them, because the "I" from which you speak is the "I" of the Witness.

You may be identifying with who you *think* you are by maintaining a disempowering role, relationship, image, thought, feeling or behavior. It is helpful to remove the filters of identification by clarifying what you are not.

You are not your image.
You are not your thoughts.
You are not your body.
You are not your mind.
You are not your feelings.
You are not your illness.
You are not your memories.
You are not your dreams.
You are not your success.
You are not your visions.
You are not your hopes.
You are not your fears.
You are not your desires.
You are not your beliefs.
You are not your judgements.
You are not your actions.
You are not your creations.

All of the above are *expressions* of you; reflections and descriptions of who you are. Refining the expressions gives you more harmony, purpose and success in your communications. Enhancing these reflections gives you greater *personal* presence, because your *impersonal* presence—or *who you really are*—will illuminate the reflection.

A Course In Miracles shares, "In this world you can become a spotless mirror—Clean but the mirror, and the message that shines forth from what the mirror holds out for everyone to see, no one can fail to understand."

> *Personal presence is the mirror.*
> *Witness is the messenger.*
> *Life purpose is the message.*

Life Purpose

Everyone has a natural yearning to know his purpose in life. Life purpose is the intangible resolution of your life that is the main message of the Witness. Witness is the messenger and the message is the life purpose. This message is the motive that generates correct thinking. It is a perfect gauge with which to monitor your actions. You can save much of otherwise wasted time if you ask yourself, "Is this activity, person, role, dialogue, friendship, job, situation, event, decision, in *accord* with my life purpose?"

Purpose fosters hope, fulfillment, self-motivation and positive intent. When you have a purpose, you can easily create goals that are positive, and you are motivated to take the necessary action to fulfill those goals. Life purpose gives you the ability to discern how you are going to devote your time and energy in your life. Our purpose is usually much bigger than we are, but it must include us. Most of all, it must be *internalized.* Then your purpose can be achieved under any circumstance.

Having a purpose in life can actually prolong your life. A study done in a convalescent home revealed the effects of having a purpose. Judith Roden of Harvard had two groups of patients for 18 months. One group had the goal of taking care of a potted plant. The other group did not have a daily goal. The former group lived twice as long as the latter. Having a goal, even one as simple as taking care of a potted plant, gave the patients a purpose to be here. My grandmother, a formidable woman 88-years-old, says that, "You simply have to *choose* to keep going and not *choose* to give up."

Purpose and worth are often confused; many people look continually outside of themselves to know their worth. When you determine your personal worth by your job, career, family, social position, income or appearance, you create a dilemma for yourself. You must constantly *work* for approval, love, acceptance and control in order to feel as if you are earning your worth and living up to that standard. If and when life throws you an unexpected curve—you lose your job, you begin to look older, your children grow up or you retire—you may find yourself feeling unneeded, even worthless; all of which is depressing. You can spend a lifetime looking *outside* to find meaning.

Life purpose comes only from within. If every individual in a family, corporation and community knew his or her life purpose, then a sense of peace, cooperation and order would reign. Much of the competitive comparing, self-seeking, coercive and manipulative behaviors would be eliminated, and everyone would feel appreciated for their *value*. When people feel the dignity of self-value, they understand the significance of the least thought, action and word. They know the power of their true self and the importance of fulfilling their life purpose.

People usually think that what they do externally will give them meaning. But, the opposite is true.

> *It is **who you are** (internally)*
> *which brings meaning to what you do.*

You give meaning to what you do. What you do does not give you meaning. It is already there. You do not have to earn it. You must only have the desire to know and seek within. Your purpose may not be revealed to you on the first inquiry, or second or third. Your desire must be great, bigger than anything else. When that happens, Witness will tell you.

We often look for work that will give us a sense of purpose. In many ways the choice of work is crucial to whether or not we can express our unique strengths, attributes and abilities. The forum in which we choose to work is our life's work, not purpose. This must not be confused. When you think that your life work will satisfy your life purpose, then you set yourself up for great anxiety and disappointment. Life purpose must be an inner commitment that can be achieved under almost any fate that befalls you. However, the mere act of defining your life purpose is strong enough to bring you such focus as to probably steer you away from poor choices and unconscious decisions.

Life work involves choosing a work environment and position that enables you to perform enjoyable functions to which you are innately attracted. There are many career development courses available to help people explore their strengths, their best mental functions, styles of learning and communication. These are areas to explore when you are seeking your life's work. Your life's work may bring you recognition because when you do what you love to do and are naturally inclined toward everyday, then you are usually successful and happy—at least secure and content. When people see that you are well suited to a position, company, career or lifestyle, they will say, "You have really found your niche in life."

But your niche in life is not your life purpose. Other people can see your inner resolve, direction, and commitment, by watching your actions, the tough choices that you make, and your courage to do what you believe in. Your life purpose is so powerful that it can override even a poor choice of life work, and come barging through to be completed under all circumstances. The message is part of your soul, merged with who you are, forming something that is much bigger than (maybe) you ever planned. You can be a vehicle for your life purpose, which is an exhilarating choice. Suggestions here are to consider it. There is no better generator of personal presence than the purpose which is much greater than yourself.

When we say that you can execute your life purpose regardless of what you do in life, this precludes committing unnatural mistreatment of others. Any and all forms of abuse are unnatural and futile acts of unconsciousness. To think of them as anything else is an irresponsible use of the mind. When you know your real self, it is impossible to harm another person without great remorse.

You have a life purpose whether you are rich or poor, famous or forgotten, old or young, male or female. No matter the color of your skin, the religion of your culture, the government which rules or serves you, you have a purpose for being here today. Whether you are a socialite, CEO, gardener, truck driver, homemaker, royalty, sales clerk, senator or a consumer of welfare and correctional services—you have a life purpose.

Inner Silence

Inner silence is the key mission of the Witness. Silence is a paradox, and not exactly what the word implies. Not unlike a sound, silence can be heard. Like a wave of energy, it can be felt. It is difficult to explain, but it has been described as the depth of peace or a state of grace. It is like an emptiness that is entirely full. You can hear it with the inner ear of your mind. Silence is a state of mind—a sense of having a quiet, humming, soothing vibration in the very center of your brain. In the stillness of your external environment, you can hear the vibrations in that space in the center.

Inner silence is a state of presence that creeps up on you sometimes, and suddenly you are "in it". You are not thinking about being in it, you are not talking about being in it, you are not waiting to be in it, you are not remembering when you were in it, you are not trying to be in it, you are not practicing to be in it, nor are you observing yourself while you are in it— *You Just Are.*

Realizing this state is of immeasurable benefit. Its gifts are bountiful and include such treasures as: Serenity, repose, calm, bliss, joy, faith, hope, trust, honesty and certainty—a formidable list.

One way to recognize this state of silence is by experiencing and knowing what it is not. It is not judging, discriminating, analyzing, worrying, seeking, hoping, desiring, dreaming, scheming or remembering. It is neither living in the past nor contemplating the future. IT IS NOW.

Be still and know. That is inner silence.

Inner silence corresponds to the mental state of NON-thinking. Yes, it is possible to not think. Actually, your finest moments in life are when you are not thinking, just *being.* Learning to be still and simply "be" requires practice, but it may be the best thing you ever learn.

Conclusion of Part One

The Witness is the source of your power of personal presence. Without this source of power, all other states of presence are in some way a misrepresentation, an imbalance, a projection that lacks truth. The image is what you appear to be, but your presence is a reflection of something much greater. You are more than you can conceive. You are a creation greater than is possible to imagine and too *expansive* to truly grasp.

To grasp it is to limit it. To limit who you are by identifying solely with who you appear to be is a choice that is made out of lack of knowledge and fear.

The courage to seek your real self within, and upon finding it, to strive to express that real self through every avenue given you: thoughts, actions, speech and appearance are parts of the process of becoming real, becoming self-empowered, and coming into your power of personal presence.

o   o   o

PART 2

The Practice Of Personal Presence

*"Whatever aid I give you will be as a grain of sand
compared to the mountains you must move for yourself."*
Og Mandino

*"By what I did yesterday I win today;
This is the virtue of practice. "*
Hoizin School of Zen

*"You must do the thing
that you think you cannot do."*
Eleanor Roosevelt

This how-to section is written in a format that makes it easy to proceed with practicing personal presence. Physical, mental, emotional and spiritual presence are covered. There are charts, forms and questions to consider, as well as practices, exercises and meditations to do.

Most significant practices and learning experiences cannot be translated to others in written form. The following are just a few that will delineate how to practically put some of the concepts in this book to use right away.

How Present Are You?

Your answers to this questionnaire will give you a sense of how present you are. The questions are separated as they relate to the physical, mental and emotional selves. If you answer "Yes" to a majority *(50 percent or more)* of these questions, then the practices of personal presence which follow the questionnaire will be very helpful to you. If you answer "No" to a majority (*more than 50 percent*) of them, then you are already practicing the techniques and presence is more or less becoming a State of Being for you.

Physical

1. Do you ever feel as if you are not really "there"?
2. Do people ever express surprise at the job you do?
3. When you tell people that you are a mother of two and a homemaker, do they respond, "Oh, I thought so?"
5. When you catch a quick look at yourself while passing a mirror, do you think or say something negative about

yourself or your appearance?

6. Do you ever let others dictate what you should wear?

7. Do you often complain to others about your body or appearance?

8. Have you ever, or are you now, waiting for some outside change to occur before you allow yourself to look your personal best?

9. Do you feel more comfortable in groups of people who are dressed similarly to your attire?

10. Do you feel more comfortable around people with similar body weight?

11. Do you have unconscious body movements, such as facial ticks, fidgety fingers, or tapping feet that happen when you feel unsettled?

12. Do people say to you that you are really quite different than their first impression of you?

13. Do people tend to not notice or recognize you?

14. Do you ever hesitate to look your best in a given situation?

15. Do you pretend that how you look doesn't matter to you?

16. Do you think that your appearance is limiting to you?

17. Do you feel that your appearance is in conflict with the role that others see

you in?

18. Do you feel that you suffer prejudice due to your clothing or appearance?

19. Do people sometimes not realize that you are in the room?

20. Do you deflect compliments about your appearance with comments like, "Oh, this old thing." or "I got it cheap at..." or "This coordination was an accident of luck," or "I am just getting older?"

21. Does it bother you if you are not perfect?

22. Do you think that you should be?

23. Do you think that your physical attractiveness is the best thing you've got?

24. Do you have a closet stuffed with clothes, with nothing really to wear?

25. Do you hate shopping?

26. Can you trust your own judgement to know if something looks good on you or not?

27. Are you uncomfortable turning around or walking ahead of others because people will look at the back of your body?

28. Do others back up when you talk to them?

29. Do you feel tension in your body that you cannot get rid of?

30. Does anyone around you complain

about your appearance?
32. Are you clumsy?
33. Are your hands and feet often cold?
34. Do you think that you could have an annoying voice tone?
35. Are you uncomfortable hugging or touching others with natural affection?
36. Does it make you uncomfortable to be hugged?
37. Do you sometimes find it difficult to breathe?
38. Does anyone ever ask you if you are angry when you are not?
39. Do you maintain habits that you know are unhealthy for your body?
40. Is your body language and/or tone of voice apologetic?
41. Do you feel your body and are you aware of how it is sitting or lying down right now while reading this?

Emotional

1. Do you often feel like crying?
2. Do you blow situations out of proportion?
3. Do you feel that others reject you frequently?
4. Are you afraid to tell the truth?
5. Are you unaware of how you feel about things?
6. Do you feel guilty when you say no?

7. Are you often misunderstood?

8. Do you have trouble communicating what you mean?

9. Do you feel that others do not believe you?

10. Do you get angry easily if things aren't going as planned?

11. Do you worry often?

12. Are you afraid that others will not like you if you are powerful?

13. Do you avoid conflict and confrontation?

14. Do you hesitate to stand up for what is right?

15. Do you feel unworthy?

16. Do you feel that others encroach on your personal space?

17. Are you uncomfortable when others know you well?

18. Do you do things that you do not want to do in order to please others?

19. Do you feel that people do not listen to you?

20. When a manager calls you into the office, do you experience a fleeting fear that you are going to be fired?

21. Do people make you feel guilty?

22. Do you believe others when they compliment you?

23. Do you procrastinate?

24. Are you disorganized?

25. Do you feel like you need to have

everything perfect?

26. Are you afraid that if you let down your guard you will lose control?

27. Do you feel defensive when someone criticizes you?

28. Do you trust your own judgement?

29. Are you confused about what others mean?

30. Do you wonder if people really like you?

31. Is it more important for you to be liked than to be yourself?

32. Do you enjoy gossip?

33. Do you want approval for everything?

34. Do you feel that you have to ask permission before you can do things?

35. Do you feel that things are not going to work out for you?

36. Are you guarded about how you really feel?

37. Do you think of some people as saps?

38. Are you prejudiced against people of other races, religions or gender?

39. Do you think that sexual harassment is overrated or baloney?

40. Is it a strain for you to smile?

41. Are you always tired?

42. Does it make you especially uncomfortable to see a woman or man cry?

43. Do you cry yourself?

44. Do you feel threatened when someone else of the same gender is attractive?

45. Do you try to hide your true feelings from others?

Mental

1. Do you find yourself hearing a story being told before you realize that you are not listening?

2. Do you mentally rework an entire conversation you had over again when you are driving your car?

3. Do you think that people are talking about you?

4. Are you full of mind chatter?

5. Do you find it difficult to meditate?

6. Do you withhold information from others that you know they could use?

7. Do you expect to achieve your goals?

8. Are you often thinking of the worst that could happen?

9. Are you unconscious of many of your thoughts?

10. Do you ever ignore your intuition?

11. Do you think that you fall short of people's expectations?

12. Do you have lists and lists of things to do?

13. Do you have a better plan of what

you think others should do?

14. Do you have difficulty admitting a mistake?

15. Do you find it difficult to apologize?

16. Do you blame others and yourself?

17. Do you rationalize most situations?

18. Do you hang around people who think like you do?

19. Do you provoke tension with your negative attitudes?

20. Are you ever obsessed with certain thoughts?

21. Are you uncomfortable being alone for very long?

22. Do you have negative thoughts about others?

23. Do you still blame your parents for your pain?

24. Do you think that *you* would never need counseling?

25. Do you need to control what everyone is doing and how they are doing it?

26. Do you have trouble delegating responsibility?

7. Do you ever judge the importance of information or opinions coming to you based on the gender of the person delivering it?

28. Do you plan what you are going to say before you have really heard the other person?

29. Do you feel anxious in everyday conversations?

30. Do you consider the time you take to converse with people whom you judge to be less competent than you, to be wasted or less important time?

31. Do you try to rationalize every interaction that occurs in your relationships until you can feel better?

32. Do you resent it when you are told what to do?

33. Do others ever call you stubborn?

34. Do you feel that you get overlooked in business arenas based on your gender?

35. Do you get anxious when you know that you are going to meet someone who you perceive to be more powerful than you?

36. Do you like to rebel against authority?

37. Do you ever say the very opposite of what you want to?

38. Do you agree with others in order to get their approval?

39. Do you ask others to do special favors that may be inconvenient to them?

40. Do you use guilt or fear of disapproval to get others to do what you want?

41. Have you ever tried to use legitimate

power to get what you want from the opposite sex ?

42. Do you frequently tell people about your education, job or social position soon after you meet them?

43. Do you discount the experience of those older than you?

44. Do you compare yourself constantly to others?

45. Do you stand your ground in important task-related matters?

46. Do people's opinions of you and your life cause you to doubt yourself?

47. Do you feel assertive?

48. Do you deny your own needs and wants so that others can have theirs?

49. Do you have trouble making decisions? Would you prefer to have others make decisions for you?

50. Do you look to see what is wrong with others?

51. Do you interrupt others when they are in the middle of a sentence? Any person *in particular*?

Spiritual

If you answer *Yes* to the majority of these, then you are communicating and identifying often with your Witness.

1. Do you feel deep moments of peace?

2. Are you in awe of the mysteries of this life?

3. Do you feel comforted even when situations are very difficult?

4. Do you have a sense that "Everything is going to be okay?"

5. Do you feel that there is a purpose to everything that happens?

6. Do you know your life purpose?

7. Are you fulfilling it right now in your life?

8. Do you like to spend time in solitude?

9. Do you meditate?

10. Do you *know* things without any external reason why?

11. Are you telepathic?

12. Do you truly respect all living beings?

13. Are you kind with yourself?

14. Do you sometimes feel the pain of the world?

15. Do your think that life is the perfect *curriculum*?

16. Do you enjoy another's success?

17. Are you compassionate?

18. Do you have prophetic dreams?

19. Do you avoid political games?

20. Do you have a conscious awareness of responsibilities?

21. Do you truly feel bad (but without harboring self-punishing habits of guilt and shame) when you speak or think

about others with disdain?

22. Do you expect miracles?

23. Do you feel certain that there is purposeful good to be found somewhere in all situations?

24. Do you look for it?

25. Do you sometimes feel a warm love within for yourself for no particular reason?

26. Are you often misunderstood, but it doesn't bother you at all?

27. Do you ever feel you are in a state of non-doing and non-thinking but getting a lot done?

28. Do you feel a peaceful awareness that you cannot put into words?

29. Do you hear a definite voice within guiding you?

30. Can the beauty of nature or music bring you to tears?

31. Do you have any particular abilities or gifts such as keen vision, interpretation of concepts or healing inclinations?

32. Do you take care to monitor and nurture these abilities?

33. Do you feel called to serve?

34. Do you experience psychic events that seem like tests?

35. Are you highly sensitive to other people's pain—physical or emotional—and feel you must help them release the

burden?

36. Is it difficult, if not impossible, for you to just shut down your heart?

37. Do you contemplate the concept of time?

38. Do you know what babies or animals are feeling and thinking?

39. Do you have vivid, colorful dreams at night?

40. Is it easier as you get older to let go of trivial frustrations?

41. Do you like to accomplish things, reach your goals, but most of all, just BE?

Goal Setting

One of the most powerful ways to achieve anything in life is through goal setting. All evidence of success in people—whether defined as having material possessions or high self-esteem—demonstrates that setting goals is IMPERATIVE for achieving results. Personal presence requires goal-setting also.

Write down the goals you have established on subjects discussed in this book. For instance self-empowerment, communication, transcending roles, silencing mind chatter, enhancing your wardrobe, posture, voice, emotional balance, etc. Each of these topics is a goal that can be reached, or a quality that is worth maintaining. You have to goal-set to do it. I suggest keeping a journal of goals with dates and expected time of achievement. A plan to maintain your goals is necessary. You may want to move with more co-ordination and grace, or want a new look for work, or want to heal your inner child. Set your vision on the goal NOW. You will learn to bring future positive energy in to the present instead of the past's negative energy. Use the present as a gifted moment of power to either heal, enhance, empower, maintain or improve yourself and your life. Goal-set for increasing positive presence in this world.

A simple format for life goals is to make a list of "100 THINGS I WANT TO DO", "100 THINGS I WANT TO HAVE" and "100 THINGS I WANT TO BE". Take three separate sheets of paper, title them accordingly and have fun by letting go and writing down all the possibilities. This type of goal brainstorming is an excellent way to shake the habit of limiting yourself, or saying that you don't know what you want. Get a clear picture of the possibilities. Then, take specifics from the list and place them in an order of preference. Use the following page as an example.

Goal Setting

Lifetime: This is your vision for your lifetime, such as a "Long, Satisfied, Happy, Healthy Life."

10 Year:

7 Year:

5 Year:

4 Year:

3 Year:

2 Year:

1 Year:

6 Month:

3 Month:

Next Month:

From the preceding list, my major goals in each category are:

Physical:_____
_____
_____
_____

Emotional:_____
_____
_____
_____

Professional:_____
_____
_____
_____

Family:_____
_____
_____
_____

Intellectual:_____
_____
_____
_____

Social:_____
_____
_____
_____

Spiritual:_____
_____
_____
_____

Physical Self

Image: Be as objective as you can in answering these questions. It may be necessary to filter out input from relatives and friends (conditioning) who may be unintentionally putting you in a box in regard to your appearance.

Am I happy with my appearance right now?
__ Never __ Sometimes __ Often
__ Most Of The Time __ Always

Why or Why not?

_____
_____
_____
_____
_____

What do I want my appearance to say about me?

_____
_____
_____
_____

(Include as many words that describe "qualities" as opposed to actual size, shape etc. Focus on the character, the inner qualities which you would like to project. Brainstorm it with a friend. Don't limit yourself at all.)

People often describe me as:

_____

_____

_____

_____

_____

Is my appearance consistent with my goals? Refer to your chart.   __Yes __ No

Explain._____

_____

_____

_____

_____

_____

Image And Roles

When you read the role-playing in Chapter Seven, you had definite images of what each role looked like, didn't you? One can appear to be a tired mother of two, or a controlled executive iron maiden, a cute bouncy cheerleader, or the ultimate femme fatale seductress. You can easily picture the fatherly type, the playboy with the gold chain or the yuppy I-have-to-always-win look. It is fun to have these looks in your wardrobe from which to pick and choose at will.

You can have one of these looks and not necessarily be playing that role. But you do not want a stereotype picture affixed in other people's mental vision of you. Do not limit yourself to clothing that exudes these roles without assuring that your speech, actions, and even thoughts are balanced. You do not want to be limited by either your habits of behavior or your wardrobe.

It is possible to have your own personal style even if you *are* a small and cute person, a mother, a CEO, a sexy guy. But you want to look empowered, not *typical* of that role. Though it is more important to change behavior, you must remember that as soon as you walk into a room, others will assess whether you are credible at what you do in life, no matter what it is.

If you had to pick from among the roles, which one do you think you most look like? Circle the role below. If you think you look like more than one, number them in sequence. It is helpful to ask a wardrobe consultant (or a least a friend) to be honest with you about this.

Father/Mother	Little Boy/Little Girl
Playboy/Seductress	Winner/Cheerleader
Superman/Superwoman	Iron Man/ Iron Maiden

Based on this, what changes do I need to make in my image for each of the above?

_____
_____
_____
_____
_____

• • •

Style

> *Style is a collection of thoughts*
> *moving in visual harmony.*

One way to study style is to go to a public place like an airport, mall, park or busy business area and take notes of what you see *that is right.* We are more conditioned to pick out the fashion don'ts. People are not always bred or trained to see what is right. Right looks harmonious, pulled together, not necessarily "matchy," individualized, balanced, well-proportioned, expressive, aware, and most of all, unpretentiously attractive. Once you discover what RIGHT looks like, you can recreate it.

Harmony is achieved when your style is discovered by linking your body style and personal taste with your *message, life purpose, and positive self concepts.* This is the whole picture—that link between the source of your image, the creator of your thoughts, the foundation of your feelings and the expression of your personal style.

Checking Self-Talk About Image

Try to catch yourself when thinking or repeating this mind chatter about your image. *Canceling* mind chatter is reviewed in the next section. Be aware of the negative thinking below and strive to stop it.

Do You Ever Say Things Like:
"I can't afford it, so it's no use trying...I will wait to look my best later...I don't want people to think I care about myself too much...I don't want others to think I am concerned about fashion; it's so phony...I am angry that society says I have to look a certain way...It makes me mad to have someone else (fashion media) dictate what I should be wearing...I don't want to appear vain...If I look like I tried too hard, people will think I don't love my natural self...I will alienate others if I look too good...People should accept me for who I am and not for what I look like...and on and on.

Perhaps you can contribute your own thoughts.

Do your ever say this? Fill in the blank.
"After I have taken care of _____
in my life, then I will concentrate on myself and how I look."

Do you think like this?
"If only I looked like that, then I would be happy."
"If only I was thin, then I would be happy."
"If I was beautiful, I wouldn't have all these problems."
"It is no use trying, because I am never going to look like that anyway."

Are you the one who says?
"I never have anything to wear."
"I don't have any clothes."
"I am sick of everything in my closet."

All of the above thoughts are negative, false programming. Some people have all the clothes but they see lack, even when there is abundance. The mind is circling around and around with negative lies which are the defense mechanism for not taking responsibility for your appearance, which is part of what you are manifesting.

> *You are not only your body,*
> *But its image*
> *Is a creation of your thinking.*

How can you play dress up while shopping?

First, before entering the store, drop any preconceived ideas about what you are going to find and just explore. Try on things you love, and some things just to make you laugh, not at yourself but what you are doing. Think of this not as a duty or something you must do, but as an escape. A lot of women use shopping as an escape, a hobby or even therapy—and the retailers know it. Shopping is a multi-billion dollar industry *worldwide*. Why fight it? Enjoy shopping by letting your inner child out to play.

When you really need to establish a powerful YOU in body image, hire a consultant. A professional not only takes the stress out of shopping, but a good one makes it fun.

Men and women "go unconscious" when they enter a shopping mall or department store or a boutique. Previously clear and focused, they soon become confused, anxious and irritable. They stop breathing until they leave the store. They say, "Aren't there some better things we could be doing?"

Watch for these unwanted tapes. They can be activated by the nature of the shopping experience itself. Some people have poor, negative memories of shopping from childhood, when the accompanying adults were anxious and running their own negative programs.

Shopping is a strong catalyst for negative reruns—especially for women. A woman knows that eventually, in order to see the garment, she will have to enter a little box of a room with hopelessly poor lighting and view herself in a three-way mirror. She will have to see herself half-dressed in her undergarments, with pantyhose or worse, a pair of white, weekend athletic socks she wore with her sweats.

As soon as she enters the dressing room, even before undressing, she notices that she needs a new hair cut or color, her skin is aging and her cellulite is increasing. This is not a good start. She quickly gets dressed to cover up her flaws, look in the mirror at the new garment, but she remains focused on those self-limiting judgements. It can take a good 30 minutes to raise herself out of this state the tape activates. If you do not think that you can harness your mental chatter, then don't look into the mirror until you have the garment on. I have never found a store with lighting that encourages anyone to look at themselves for longer than a few seconds. Perhaps it is the fast-shop-spend, not fast-food strategy.

When you apply makeup you have to look at yourself. You can examine your skin, your face at close range, as well as your feelings. This is an opportunity to look yourself straight in the eye. You get to really SEE yourself. Perhaps this is why so many women apply their makeup in the rear view mirrors of their cars while sitting at a stoplight! They only have to see bits of face at a time and can avoid the whole picture.

A psychologist once told me that it is impossible for people to actually see what their bodies look like realistically and objectively. Consider this an advantage.

Men and women have been conditioned differently. After working with hundreds of men and women, I have found that men seem to generally think that they look better than they do, while women generally think that they should look better or "never look good enough."

For example, men will look at a poorly fitting garment and comment that the suit style, quality, or cut is not up to his standards. Women will often look at a poorly fitting garment and comment that *her body* style and shape is not up to her standards. This occurs regardless of a her size and shape.

Shopping Strategy

A.) *Look good when you go shopping.* This is an important time, because your time is important. Don't roll out of bed on Saturday morning, throw on some jeans or sweats, socks and sneakers and run to the mall to find that perfect business suit you needed *yesterday.* It may not be a healthy experience. If you are shopping for a suit, wear a shirt/blouse so that you can try jackets on without going into the dressing room.

B.) *Wear a garment you love for which you often receive compliments.* Then, when a salesperson compliments you on how you look, you will more readily accept the compliment. Also, when you turn the corner into the dressing room you will avoid the thought, "I hate this thing I am wearing". If there is anything you currently wear, which you dislike that much, give it away or throw it out.

C.) *Look well groomed.* You will be looking into the mirror frequently. Bring along a comb/brush and some makeup to dab on because the mirrors are usually dim and yellow, which washes out the color of your skin. Wear attractive undergarments.

D.) *Affirm:* "Shopping is easy for me. I am important. My appearance is a creative expression of my inner self. I am learning to style my look with ease and pleasure."

E.) *Hire a consultant* or make an appointment with a personal shopper—a complimentary service available in most department stores—to get you started.

F.) *Assume that the style is wrong for you, not that you are wrong for the style.* No one looks good in every style and cut, fashion models included. A quick glance at the television show, *Style,* on CNN on Saturday morning proves that.

G.) *Compliment yourself mentally.* Silently say nice things to yourself while you are shopping.

H.) *Remember that this is a creative process.* Do not think about it as much as *let it flow.* Your fingers and eyes can more easily find an attractive garment without your mind chattering away. How do you think a painter paints, a musician plays music, a dancer dances? They give their work a critical analysis *after* the the creative time is completed. During the creative process it would only block the flow.

I.) *Take risks and try on something new.* Sometimes I have to tell a client, "Just stop your judgements for a moment, and try this on." Often, amazed and delighted, they look fabulous and say, "I would never have even picked this off the rack". Begin to trust and try new things.

Accepting Acknowledgement

When you express and empower yourself, you receive compliments that are well deserved and sincerely meant. It is very important to accept them graciously and own them as true. There are many insidious ways of negating yourself by shoving compliments aside with come-backs like: "Oh, this old thing. Do you know how old this is?", or, "It is a miracle I got it all together today!", or, "This was really cheap too", "I got in on sale at —", or, "Do you really think so?" (as if you don't believe them), and so on.

This is purely a final means of self sabotage after generating all that positive energy. Women can easily confuse self-acknowledgement and dignity with humility and self-denigration. I have noticed some people who literally stop breathing when they receive a compliment. If it is just too much to handle, think about it this way:

> *When you reject someone's compliment, you are rejecting their loving support. You can either insinuate that they are lying or believe them. Accepting a compliment is not only self-loving, but it also acknowledges the giver for their kindness. Believing them shows respect for their opinion.*

Consider that when you are presenting your personal best, you are actually honoring the people in your presence. Your appearance, at any given time, is one indication of how important that person or event may be to you. Look carefully at when, where and with whom you choose to be at your best.

Some people present their best with strangers, more than with the people they love the most. This is an attitude of "Since that person already accepts and loves me, I can just look like a slob." This is a mistake. Are not those people that you love, and who love you most, the very ones who are supporting you to reach your goals?

Impression Management Chart

There are no *wrong* looks, just *incomplete* looks.

Complete	Incomplete
Finished	Unfinished
Polished	Rough around the edges
Powerful	Weak
Comfortable	Uncomfortable
Enhanced personal style	Unconscious of personal style
Talks her walk	Can't carry off the look
Visible	Invisible
Respects protocol	Inappropriate dress for occasion
Neat and clean	Unkempt, slovenly and unclean
Attention to detail	Indifferent to appearance
Balance (less is more) makeup	Overdone (tacky) makeup
Color harmony and balance	Color disharmony, imbalance
Healthy hair, individual cut and style	Damaged hair, poor cut and style
Radiant skin	Dull, unhealthy skin
Clear eyes	Lifeless eyes
Proportioned accessories	Over and under accessorized
Understated elegance	Blatant display of wealth
Well-groomed fingernails	Ungroomed fingernails

If I worked with an image consultant today,
what are the questions I would like to have answered?

_____
_____
_____
_____
_____
_____
_____
_____
_____
_____
_____
_____
_____
_____
_____
_____
_____
_____
_____
_____
_____
_____
_____
_____
_____
_____
_____
_____

Body Language

Self-limiting behavior contributes to feelings and projections of inferiority. An apologetic presence is expressed with body language like slapping your forehead, shrugging your shoulders, and verbally by apologizing for the smallest things that do not hurt anyone else.

An apologetic presence has self-effacing gestures that say:
a. I am sorry that I am here.
b. I am sorry for what I am saying.
c. I am sorry to bother you with my presence.
d. Please don't look at me.

Things Not To Do

a. Incessant smiling is a fear of not smiling or smiling as a cover up.
b. Incessant talking and interrupting others.
c. Slumped shoulders and arms crossed: Looks and sounds tired, scared and depressed.
d. Improper breathing: Voice says "I am not really here.", "I'm anxious" or "I'm scared."
e. Conspicuous grimacing and head shaking says "I am not sure of this, but..."
f. Taking up too much space, encroaching on others' body boundaries.

Body Language

Empowering	Disempowering
Dynamic relaxation	Nervous, uptight
Aligned	Misaligned
Centered	Off-center
Grounded	Ungrounded
Balanced (stands on own two feet)	Imbalanced
Relaxed muscles	Tight muscle groups
Quiet back	Tension
Heart-centered	Armored heart
Heart-mind connected	Disconnection of feelings
Body-mind connected	Ignores body sensations, numb
Graceful, dignified	Clumsy, uncoordinated
Flexible, spontaneous	Stiff, rigid
Keeps head on straight	Cocked head (tilted)
Looks straight in the eyes	Avoid direct eye contact
Strong handshake	Weak, wimpy handshake
Fullness of breath	Shallow breath patterns
Body energy flows	Out of body, all in head
Genuine expression	Smiles as a cover-up
Sincere response	Laughing when you didn't get it
Respectful encouragement	Nodding others on when they speak
Moderate hand movements	Nervous or no hand movements
No unconscious hand movements	Constant fussing with hair or face

Grounding And Alignment

The two major components of an empowered body movement and the key to creating a safe body boundary are *grounding and alignment.*

Alignment is a centering process and works together with grounding to allow the greatest amount of free flowing energy in your body. The phrase "stand up straight" is not conducive to a flexible back, and the spontaneity of movement that comes with correct alignment.

Movement and exercise GROUNDS you, and grounding creates safety in movement. Grounding occurs when you are aligned, breathing fully, and are slightly bending your knees (no locked knees.) This position allows your mental energy to drop down into your body, bringing your thoughts to the present. You immediately become more relaxed and aware of your inner self and your surroundings. When people get grounded in my exercise class, there is an instant recognition that it is not only okay to let go of tension, but that it is a very easy process.

Being HERE and NOW in your body is the most powerful point from which to move through your life. This is literally getting centered.

Study the diagram.

BODY ALIGNMENT

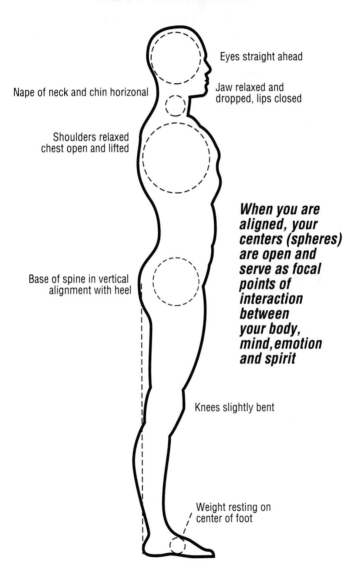

Eyes straight ahead

Nape of neck and chin horizonal

Jaw relaxed and dropped, lips closed

Shoulders relaxed chest open and lifted

Base of spine in vertical alignment with heel

When you are aligned, your centers (spheres) are open and serve as focal points of interaction between your body, mind, emotion and spirit

Knees slightly bent

Weight resting on center of foot

Now, check your own alignment. Be near a mirror, so you can check your alignment with the diagram. You may find this easier to do if you record this section aloud on an audio tape, and then play it back while following the instructions:

First face the mirror, so you can get into feeling this. Stand up. Relax. Place your feet straight ahead and shoulder width apart. Arms hanging down by your sides. Look straight ahead. Make sure that your head is squarely positioned with your chin neither too high or too low, with your eyes looking squarely straight ahead.

Think about your back as being expanded and lengthened in space. See and feel it being lifted and filled with energy. You may even envision it being filled with light. Feel as if you have a string in the middle of your head, and someone above you is pulling the string and stretching you gently upward. This takes pressure and weight off the pelvis, and gives it flexibility of movement. Slightly bend your knees to be sure you are not locking them back. Breathe deeply. Feel like your chest is a sphere of air hovering in space, light and easy. Relax your shoulders. Lift the sphere in your chest so that it is centered directly over your pelvis. You may have to tilt this imaginary sphere forward, but in most cases, people have to tilt it backward, while lifting **up** in front. Feel this lifting from the inside. Breathe fully from the chest. Relax your shoulders again. Now again think of the string lifting and stretching you up from the middle of your head. Do not force anything. Relax your arms and hands. Relax your jaws, letting them drop down, so that your teeth do not touch, keeping your lips closed, and let the tip of your tongue slightly touch the roof of your mouth at a center point behind your teeth.

Focus now on the pelvis. Notice your coccyx (the lowest tip of the spinal column, or the tail bone). It should be directly in vertical alignment with your heels, as if someone could draw a straight line from your heels up to the tip of your spine. This will make the center of the pelvis rest in perfect alignment. Imagine a sphere within the pelvis space that is centered perfectly in alignment with the chest sphere. Now you can get grounded.

Breathe into the pelvis, bending the knees slightly another inch or two, keeping yourself comfortable. You will feel your thigh muscles which should be kept relaxed, though they are contracted. Feel the gravity force between your pelvis, feet and the ground. Feel the magnetic pull. Check again that your coccyx bone is in alignment with your heels, and that your chest is centered over your pelvis.

Next, check your neck by lengthening it even more. Imagine a sphere within the head space that is centered directly over the chest and pelvis spheres. Most people carry their heads too far forward, or slightly tilted back, breaking the flow of energy just at the nape of the neck. If that is the case, bring your chin down to be in alignment with the nape of your neck. See the dotted line on the diagram. This will put your ears upright and align your eyesight with the world. You will be able to link the communication between your head, your heart, and the rest of your body more keenly (this is what we often avoid, because it brings up some feeling that is uncomfortable). Relax the shoulders, hands, jaws and face and eyeballs.

Now, turn so that you can observe this alignment in the mirror from the side. This is tricky since the head turns, but try to keep the head centered as you turn it to look. Notice that your chin is tilted down more than usual. Keep breathing. Notice where your body does not want to comply with your directions. This is where you will sense a block. Now turn straight into the mirror and keep breathing and centering the three spheres. Again relax. Notice the brightness of your eyes and how much more radiant and clear they are.

After you have learned abdominal breathing in the next section, follow the instruction on alignment again while breathing abdominally. This is deeply relaxing, centering and grounding.

When you have practiced *standing* still in alignment, go on to other movements in alignment:

1.   *Walk in this alignment.* Feel yourself flow through space. Be aware of your thoughts.

2.   *Run in alignment, especially outdoors.* This will greatly improve your speed and endurance and beautify your form. A lot of energy is wasted in even a slightly off-centered line in the body in movement.

3.   *Work out in alignment.* This is very important especially if you are working with weights and Nautilus. There are new machines designed to keep your body in perfect alignment while lifting. Some bodies are well endowed with muscles which are

misaligned—so the power is there, but the grace is lost.

4. *Dance in alignment.* There is probably no other medium more spontaneous, free and graceful. Dance was once a spiritual practice, and can be one again.

5. *Meditate in alignment.* The body/mind connection is facilitated through meditation, which can only be done correctly when the body centers are aligned. An aligned body is more open to an aligned heart, mind and spirit.

When you are aligned, you physiologically experience your spheres or centers as focal points of interaction between your body, mind, and spirit.

This is literal. These centers must be aligned physically in order to be functioning well, *energetically*, allowing natural vitality, rejuvenation, coordination and grace to flow.

Voice

Rhythm of speech is formed by tone, articulation and vocabulary. Tape yourself in a conversation with a friend, reading a script or with your family during dinner. Then listen and note the rhythm of your speech. Ask a friend to be honest with you about whether or not you speak too much, too quickly or too slowly and monotonously.

Steps To Empower Your Voice

1. Lower the pitch
2. Speed up or slow down in rhythm,

whichever you need to do.

3. Breathe fully and with connected rhythm by practicing the breath awareness in the last section.

4. Relax your face, jaw and throat, stand in alignment and get grounded.

5. Get willing and ready to be heard. You deserve it!

Do you have an appropriate rhythm?

Not varying your pace, pitch and volume to suit what you are saying affects your presence. If you do not have a good rhythm established for what you are saying, then you may catch others nodding off, looking at their watches, interrupting you, nodding for you to get on with it or having a glazed expression. This may happen because you have terrible listening skills and are uncomfortable being present. However, make sure that people's apparent disengagement from you is not due to your own rhythm of speech.

Do you have a disagreeable and disempowering tone, such as those below?

1. Whining
2. Sing-song
3. Monotone
4. Mumbling
5. Whispering
6. Ending always on the down pitch, nasality
7. Inane giggling
8. Twangs

9. Heavy ethnic phonations
10. Speaking too slowly: Others will try to finish your sentences, then you won't feel heard.
11. Speaking too fast: Makes others feel anxious.
12. Not breathing between sentences prevents people from a chance to comment.

Any of the above expresses the following:
"Don't expect too much from me because I have not grown up yet."
"I am not worth listening to."
"I am really not very smart, so I am probably wrong about this."
"I am afraid, sad, depressed and boring."
"I am unsure of myself."
"I am never happy with anything because nothing is ever good enough."
"Nobody ever listens to me in meetings. People always interrupt me."

Empowering Tone

1. Lowering the pitch is the most credible action and carries conviction, authority and power.
2. A nice change of rhythm between high, medium and low between words.
3. The voice comes from the center of the body, and is empowered by a calm

breathing pattern and relaxed body.

Disempowering Vocabulary

Trying to qualify every statement to avoid sounding harsh, or in a woman's case, unfeminine.

1. Ending a sentence with "don't you think?"
2. "Sorta" or "like this", "It was sorta like—."
3. Use of fillers such as : "Um, Er , Uh, ya know, an-da—ab-da"—.
4. "This is kinda how we do it"
5. Adding "just" or "really" to every adjective such as the pattern of "fashion talk" at a social function where everything is <u>just</u> divine, <u>too</u> fabulous, and <u>really</u> marvelous. All it says is, "We all know on the inside that this is a superficial occasion and holds no true power, so let's don't get into anything too deep, okay? Overly dramatic speech is characteristic of insecure and superficially directed people, so be careful to avoid coming across that way.
6. Avoiding straightforward statements for fear of scaring others off. A straightforward direct statement is reassuring to most people and it lends a definite air of credibility. This is true especially when you are saying, "Sorry, I am accountable for that mistake" which is much more empowering than hedging around by saying "sorta, kinda, don't know, maybe, could have had something to do with me." The fastest way to end the embarrassing and uncomfortable feeling of being in error is to quickly and precisely admit it so that you can immediately focus on the solution.
7. Failing to take credit for accomplishments such as :

"After the business plan was written," instead of "After I completed designing the business plan," or "After it was done," instead of, "After I did it." Or: "When the project team was formulated," instead of "After we formulated the project team."

8. "Should" statements which imply arrogance or judgement.

9. Overly formal, fancy statements are annoying as if you are trying to appear sophisticated or superior.

Active Listening

Active Listening is the key to:
1. Understanding
2. Intimacy
3. Learning who you really are and what you think. (You have to listen to your own mind too.)
4. Relaxing others in your presence
5. Maintaining relaxation yourself
6. Being able to respond instead of react.

Steps To Active Listening
1. Still your mind chatter.
2. Breathe fully and connectedly.
3. Erase body history.
4. Body awareness.
5. Let there be silence.
6. If you need to clarify something, or must interrupt, ask before cutting in.
7. First respond to what you have heard, then present your own ideas if you want to redirect the focus.

Emotional Presence

Forgiveness is an act of power that opens space around you and everyone else in your life. Forgiveness relieves you of the past and rewards you with the present. Your forgiveness opens the possibility for others around you to forgive.

Every time you forgive, look at yourself in the mirror. You will see how much clearer and happier you look, not to mention how free you feel. Forgiveness gives your cheeks a healthy glow. Any time you let go of mental blocks and open your heart, your blood can flow more freely from the heart to the head.

Forgiveness is acting from your power center, instead of sitting in victim consciousness. If you think it is more important to be forgiven than it is to forgive, then you are in victim consciousness. You could be waiting around for a long time. Your *action* is what brings about the opening. This is *your* power.

Forgiveness, however painful it can be to accomplish, is always a pleasurable result on all levels. It is opening, outgoing, healing, warming, expanding and empowering. This is wonderful for your personal presence.

First let us start with self-forgiveness because it is you who is primarily affected by it. It is difficult to forgive others when there is underlying self-judgment and guilt. Make any affirmation that is significant to you. Choose from one of the following or write your own. Write the affirmation 100 times. After each line, write just below that affirmation your immediate subconscious response to this sentence. As you do this, be aware of your body feelings, emotions and your thoughts in reaction to the affirmation. Keep going until you feel a breakthrough. It is best not to generalize but to forgive specific instances concerning specific people.

Breathe fully and deeply. This is wonderful self-therapy.

I forgive myself.

I forgive myself for not forgiving myself earlier.

I forgive myself for holding onto resentments in my mind, heart and body.

I forgive myself for not forgiving myself earlier.

The Walk of Innocence

A wonderful way to forgive self and others is to go on a *Walk Of Innocence*. You will want to be alone, and go on a hike for a whole day, or at least three to four hours. If you are prohibited in any way from getting out alone in the outdoors, then find a good spot by a window and watch the sky.

As you are walking or sitting, begin to go back in time, and remember all the incidents for which you are harboring a memory of pain and resentment. If your memory recalls a bad feeling from the past which has not changed for the better, that is your clue that you have not forgiven this person. Do not just generalize, and clump everything together about one person, say a former husband, or wife, a sibling, a daughter or son, a mother or father. Touch on the *specific instances* for which you need to forgive that person. You may spend a long time just on one person. Go ahead. Spend as long as necessary, even if it is many days. Once you get the mind set of letting go, then you will begin to breeze through. It is so liberating to realize that you do not have to walk around with these bad feelings bottled up inside anymore. That in itself can bring up the grief over the loss of a kind of relationship which you both needed and wanted, but never had. Grieve the loss. It will set your heart free for the future.

> *Anyone from your past for whom you hold*
> *resentments is walking around inside of you.*

You are a worthy forgiver. Do not underestimate the power of this process. As you forgive in your heart you are liberated. You learn that you do not have to DO anything in order to be loved. You no longer have to prove that you are worthy of love and forgiveness. You just have to open up and let it go.

Affirm: Specific affirmation for the following fears:

1. Fear of success.
It is safe for me to succeed.
2. Fear of failure.
There is no such thing as failure for me.
3. Fear of change—fear of the unknown.
Change is empowering and safe for me.
4. Fear of visibility—being seen
It is safe for me to be seen.

5. Fear of responsibility.
Responsibility is freedom and gives me choices.
7. Fear of criticism—being wrong
It is safe for me to know I am approved of and powerful at the same time.

Healing Processes

1. Inner child work
2. Breath therapy
3. Movement and dance therapy
4. Hypnotherapy
5. Dream journaling
6. Ceremony/drumming/chanting
7. Prayer/fellowship
8. Art and massage therapy
9. Hatha Yoga and martial arts
10. Meditation

Mental Presence

Canceling Negative Thinking: People are talking to themselves all the time. They use phrases like: "I am ugly; I hate being here; I am angry, I am sick and tired of this; I can't do it; I am stupid," and on and on and on. These are debilitating chants which will definitely manifest in your life, so that you can be proven right. Don't do this to yourself. If you find yourself in a deluge of negative self-talk, you must (a.) recognize it, (b.) release it, (c.) cancel it, and (d.) reverse it to a positive.

Each time your mind declares (accepts) an unwanted statement, it manifests in you or in your experience. It is important to harness your thoughts by releasing, canceling and reversing the negative phrases. As an example: When you (a.) recognize the thought, "I am getting sick," follow these steps: (b.) "I release the thought that I am getting sick," (c.) "I *(cancel)* am *(cancel)* getting *(cancel)* sick *(cancel)*. and, (d.) "I am healthy right now."

Determine which role you most often agree to play and see below which one is more likely to be invested in wanting approval or wanting control:

Wants Approval	Wants Control
Mother/Father	Seductress/Playboy
Little Girl/ Little Boy	Iron Maiden/ Iron Man
Cheerleader/Winner	Superwoman/Superman

Then work with the following affirmations:

I am willing to give up wanting approval.
I am willing to give up wanting control.
Since it is safe for me to be powerful and present, I can now give up wanting approval and wanting control.

Silencing Mind Chatter

1. Breathe in a relaxed, connected rhythm, keeping your lower abdomen "soft". If you feel it tighten up, then you are tensing up with thoughts.

2. Relax the jaw and allow the breath to flow freely.

3. Let your awareness "drop" down into the center of your body, as low as the abdomen.

4. Become aware of the subtle "impulses" of energy and movement in your body, and allow your body to gently follow that energy flow.

5. When you do this, you will notice that your thoughts have slowed down.

6. Ask yourself a question that is impossible to answer, like, "What did I look like before I was conceived?"

7. Listen to the sounds around you come alive. Enjoy the peace of mind.

The Process of Non-thinking

1. Focusing the mind or bringing your thoughts to a still-point, by repeating a single word, such as One. Slowly draw out the word for the entire length of your exhale.

2. Allowing your thoughts to flow without strain or judgement, but always coming back to the still point.

3. Breathe in and out in a connected way, focusing on air passing to and from your nostrils. Be aware of the cool feeling on the inhale and the warm feeling of the breath on the exhale.

4. You are aware that you are in a state of deep relaxation.

5. You are meditating—which means that you are in a state of deep concentration and are not consciously thinking "I am now in this state of meditation," but you are not asleep, neither are you in

the process of bringing your thoughts to a still point. Do this for at least 20 minutes.

Mental Rehearsal

This is an exercise in creative imagination. You can rehearse any event that you want to create. Have a positive expectation of successful manifestation. Get in a comfortable setting with little to no distractions. Now, imagine something that you want to happen in the future—say, you are speaking dynamically in front of a group, you are winning an award for an achievement, or you are exloring the pyramids in Egypt. You can either see yourself as if you were in a movie, or you can be inside of your future self and visualize looking down at your body which is in motion experiencing the event. Now, imagine as many details as possible. What are you doing, wearing, feeling, saying? The more you can sense the whole experience the better. Use what you see, hear, feel, touch, taste and smell. By doing this, you will notice that you are physiologically experiencing a future event *in the now.* It is effective to visualize your clothing also, and even better if you already own it. When you are actually in the experience, you will look down and remember the event of your mental rehearsal. Your body will physiologically respond with the personal presence that is in perfect syncronization with your surroundings.

The Breath

Belly Breath: This breathing is the natural breathing pattern you do when you are sleeping. It requires the least effort when you have learned how to make it a subconscious response as well as a conscious discipline. Animals are always breathing fully into the body like this, except when they are alerted by a strange sound, or stalking a prey (they hold their breath at that moment). The full breath is relaxing, and more importantly, *grounding*. This gets you fully *here* in your body, *now*. You may notice your body resisting the flow of this breath by trying to push it along. Practice relaxing into the breath and you will get the feeling of *letting life breathe through you.*

When you breathe as if you are relaxed, you will become relaxed. Give yourself permission to enjoy the deep states of relaxation which occur when you breathe in this natural, uncontrolled, rhythm.

To start, sit comfortably in a chair with back aligned. Relax. Inhale and exhale through the nose, shifting your breathing to the lower abdomen. Notice the rise and fall of your abdomen. Spend a few moments breathing naturally this way. Then exhale fully. Contract the lower abdomen slightly to push out any excess air. Now, inhale, *filling the lower abdomen* (the belly will let go, relax and fill out like a balloon) with air, then slowly filling and rising up through the diaphragm, chest, and on up through to the top of the throat, where it connects with the nostrils. Try not to let the shoulders tense up or lift. Let the air rise up through your body, with your torso surrendering to the movement of the breathing.

Next, exhale, without pushing, letting go with complete relaxation until you have emptied all but the last bit in the lower abdomen. Begin immediately with the next inhalation from the lower abdomen. The cycle is full, connected and relaxed.

Breath Focusing

These breathing rhythms teach you appreciation of the power of the breath over your feelings and thoughts.

1.   Breathe like the above while counting. Inhale to count of 4, hold for count of 16, exhale to count of 8.

Inhale 4, hold 16, exhale 8.

If this is too difficult try a 3-12-6 pattern—inhale for 3 counts, hold for 12 counts, exhale for 6 counts.

When these are comfortable for you, increase the count to a 5-20-10 pattern.

2.   Hold right nostril shut with finger, pressing lightly so that no air enters on the inhale through that side. Inhale 5 counts, exhale 10 counts.

Do this twenty times (you will be inhaling and exhaling out of the right nostril only).

3.   Hold left nostril.

Inhale 5 counts exhale 10 counts. You will be inhaling and exhaling out of the left nostril only. When you feel you can increase the count —do in 6, out 12, then in 7 and out 14.

Do each nostril 20 times each. *Always* do both nostrils in the same sitting. This is because of the effects this breathing has on the right and left hemispheres of the brain, which should be stimulated equally for balance.

Alternate Breathing: Holding the right nostril shut with your finger, breathe in through left nostril. At the top of the inhale, change fingers and close off the left nostril, exhaling through the right. Keep finger on left nostril, while you inhale in the right side, change fingers, and exhale on the left side—repeat from the beginning. Do this 20 times. If you practice this daily for one month you will rapidly develop a relationship with your breath that will teach you many things. Breathe in the breath of life.

Connected Breathing: This is a life-transforming breathing technique. During this rejuvenating therapy, the breath is so powerfully connected with the mind and spirit that all unwanted negative mental mass is exposed rapidly. Exhalation is the body's major method of releasing toxins. Negativity in mind, body and emotions is toxic to your life. This breathing pattern is best initially explored with the assistance and support of a qualified counselor. (If you do not know of one in your area look for techniques called rebirthing and holotropic breathwork.)

You can practice this alone, but do not breathe for longer than five minutes this way or for a count of 20 connected breaths. The technique is done lying down, with a full open mouth, drawing the breath into the upper chest, then immediately letting go without any breaks on the exhale. It is cathartic until you have become accustomed to living with more positive aliveness. When you have experienced this process over a period of time, you will be able to practice connected breathing underwater with a snorkel in your own bath tub. Add a cup of epsom salts for a fabulous 20 to 30 minutes rejuvenating experience. Your skin afterwards is radiant and you are vibrant due to the intense oxygenation. This simple technique helps your mental and emotional clarity.

Witness Meditation

Record your voice reading aloud the following dialogue onto a tape. Then get in a comfortable position, listen to the tape and experience it. This meditation is very empowering, helps you receive communication from the Witness and resolve problems in all your relationships. You will merge with your Witness and experience your future self in the now. It is especially good for maintaining a loving communication with yourself as well as a method of slowly uncovering your life purpose. Repeat this meditation many times.

Get into a comfortable position either lying down or sitting, making sure that your back is straight, your legs uncrossed, and arms relaxed at your side, with your hands resting on your thighs. Begin to notice your breath. Follow your breathing in and out of your nostrils, noticing the coolness of the breath on the inhale, and the warmth of the breath on the exhale.

With every exhale notice that your body is becoming more and more relaxed. Your body knows when it is just the right time to let go, and let it be completely supported.

Every muscle beginning with your toes is letting go of tension, now the ankles, calves, knees, thighs, hips and lower back, all are melting into a state of deep inner relaxation and comfort. With every breath, you are letting yourself sink into a deep, deep comfort. Now your upper back, shoulders, arms and hands are relaxing, every muscle, every cell is letting go of tension which is no longer needed. Your neck, throat, mouth and jaws are relaxing, letting go now. Relax your eyeballs, forehead, ears and scalp. Relax your brain as if it were a muscle.

Now take three deep full breaths, and see yourself in your mind's eye going into a theater. You feel very relaxed, calm, and safe. You are anticipating an interesting show. As you enter the theater you feel the slight change of temperature and the theater is darker, but your body and eyes adjust to the room quickly and comfortably. There are many chairs in rows to choose from. You are there in solitude, for this is your own special private showing, and you can pick the perfect spot.

As you sit down you realize that you are the observer who is there to witness your other three selves: moving self who is physical, thinking self who is mental, and feeling self who is emotional. You, as the Witness, are observing these three selves that are you, and how they communicate to others on the stage of your life right now. Breathing now deeply and fully you, the Witness, settle down into a chair, getting very comfortable, waiting for the show to begin.

Now the curtains before you open and reveal a stage, and on that stage you see yourself in your personal life—you and your relationship with yourself. What are you doing there on the stage? How do you feel right now? What are you thinking? How is your body moving and feeling?

Continue breathing and send waves of love from you, the Witness, to these your selves. Send them a special message of encouragement. *(Pause a minute.)* Tell them how much you love each of them there on the stage. Say, I love you. Tell them that you are always there to guide, comfort, and direct them and that you will support them in staying open to hearing you.

Now you notice that the stage is revolving, and as it turns you see yourself again on the stage, this time in your family environment. There are specific family members there with you. How are you feeling? How are you interacting with them? How is your body moving? How are you thinking? How are your thinking, feeling, and moving selves communicating with your family members?

Now breathe deeply again and let Witness communicate to them through the thinking, feeling, moving self. What does Witness want to say to them— to each one in your family? Take your time with each member, and speak to them in your mind. Witness has a message for them. What would you, the Witness, like to communicate to them, *through* the thinking, feeling and moving selves. If you need to resolve something, take a moment to let go of the problem. It is easy for the Witness, your true self, the observer of this all, to let go. *(Pause a minute.)*

Now, you see the stage revolving, and you are there again on the stage, this time in your work environment. Who is there? How are you thinking, feeling and moving? What is it that you would like to say from your Witness to each of your co-workers. What would you, the Witness, like to communicate to your co-workers *through* the thinking, feeling and moving selves? What message do you have for them? Send messages of appreciation and support. If you have a problem with someone, begin to let it go. Letting go is easy for the Witness. Resolution is natural. *(Pause a minute)*.

Now you notice that the stage is revolving, and as it turns you see yourself again on the stage, this time in your social environment; certain friends and acquaintances are there with you. How are you feeling? How are you interacting with them? How is your body moving? How are you thinking? How are your thinking, feeling, and moving selves communicating socially?

Now breathe deeply again and let Witness communicate to them through the thinking, feeling, moving self. What does Witness want to say to each one in your social environment? Take your time with each member, and speak to them in your mind. Witness has a message for them. What would you, the Witness, like to communicate to them, *through* the thinking, feeling and moving selves. If you need to resolve something take a moment to let go of the problem. It is easy for the Witness, your true self, to let this go.

Now, the stage is revolving again and the stage has turned full circle. You are there in solitude—you with yourself on the stage. Something about you is different. Your future self is there, which is very connected, centered and at One on every level of being. You are aware, following your life plan and sense your life purpose unfolding. Your Witness goes up to the stage and hugs your other three selves, deeply, lovingly and freely. You feel yourself, your Witness, *merge now* with your thinking, feeling and moving self. You are deeply aware of each part, and how each part plays a significant role in making up your personality. You are keenly aware that the real you, the Witness, is within and that you are the impersonal voice, the authentic message of who you really are. And you are expressing Witness easily, confidently, with a flow, a knowing.

You feel the truth within you. Your body is grounded, centered, aligned and moves authentically in rhythm to your inner Witness. Your emotions are balanced and filled with a powerful resource of creativity, aliveness and rejuvenation. Your mind is calm, silent, focused and directed toward positive goals. You feel a rightness about life, about you, about your world.

Now, you come down off the stage and turn around and watch the curtains closing. You feel complete. And you know that you can return and communicate like this any time you want. Taking three deep breaths, you are walking toward the exit door of the theater. Feeling secure, strong, centered and alert. Counting from five to one, you are breathing fully, and when you come to one, you will be back in the room where you began—refreshed, alert, and relaxed:

Five...Four...Three...Two...One.

Take a moment to remain peaceful and reflect on what happened during the meditation. If you like, write down the experience in a journal and keep recording your experience each time you journey within to merge with Witness.

Answer the following questions in your journal:

What were all the messages you had for your other selves and for other people during meditation? Be specific for each.

Can you see a significant message weaving throughout all your communications?

What is it?

This message is a clue to or a part of your life purpose. In time, as you go on this journey, your life purpose will become clear to you.

Affirmations

Affirmations must always be written in the present tense. You can benefit by simply reading these aloud, while staying focused. You may feel interesting sensations in your body, or hear some self-talk trying to distract you or negate the affirmation. Persist, and stay relaxed. Breathing is very important. Take a breath with every affirmation you read. You may also record the affirmations below onto a tape, and listen to them just before going to sleep at night. Lie down, relax each part of your body, take three deep breaths, turn on the tape and listen in a twilight state. Include any of your own specific affirmations as well, making sure to keep them in the present tense.

I envision a happy and successful life right now.
It is easy for me to set goals.
I expect to reach the goals that I set for myself.
I support others in reaching their goals.
I empower others and they empower me.
I affirm a positive presence today.
My presence is positive no matter what the circumstances around me.
Affirmations are easy for me to remember.
I think about my affirmations everyday, whatever I am doing.
I easily concentrate, focus and relax when I take time for myself.
I am a high achiever at work and I am balanced and relaxed at the same time.
I reach my financial goals and enjoy the process at the same time.
I am balanced and aware.
I am centered and free of tension.
I feel free because I choose the actions to take in my life.
My affairs are orderly and easy to handle.
I am organized.
I am grounded.
It is safe for me to follow my own path.
I am my true self more and more every day.
The more I am ME, the more approval and support I receive from others.
I am willing to be here and present, now.
I know my purpose.

My presence is purposeful.
I know where I am going.
I am worthy.
I am flexible.
I am strong.
It is safe for me to be powerful.
There is enough of everything for me now.
I move through life with ease.
I am safe in the world. I am wanted and loved.
I am open to new ideas.
I nurture myself.
I am willing to be supported.
It is safe for me to heal.
I let go and let God. I am ready to feel life fully.
It is safe for me to let go of pain.
I am always moving, changing, growing in aliveness.
Changing is easy for me.
I am disciplined.
I am in the dance of life, and I take my part in it.
My strength gives me freedom.
I reach my goals.
I accomplish my tasks with ease.
I have endurance, strength, and power.
I allow my body to be powerful and healthy.
I am energized for life.
I trust life.
It is safe to be here.
It is safe for me to be open to life.
It is safe for me to trust.
It is safe for me to receive.
It is safe for me to feel pleasure.
It is safe for me to be me.

I am innocent.
I forgive the past.
I feel the radiance in my whole body.
I send thoughts of love to my body every day.
I am vibrantly aware of my surroundings.
I am willing to learn from my mistakes. They are opportunities to learn.
I leave no hurt behind me, I release it!
My instincts are safe and knowing.
I love LIFE!
I am free to be me.
I am dynamically relaxed and alive.
My past supports me now.
I breathe freely and easily.
I relax with every breath I take.
I know what I need, and I give it to myself.
It is safe to be a woman(man).
I am nurturing and supportive.
I give to myself, as I give to others.
I am powerful.
I store energy for use in the future.
I am a master of my emotions.
I am balanced.
I am willing to give up wanting control and wanting approval.
I am powerful and approved of at the same time.
I create my reality.
I am no longer a victim of anything, I claim my power as a woman (as a man).
I participate in all of life.
I am 100 percent accountable for everything that happens now and this thought sets me free.

It is safe for me and everyone else around me for me to be in my power.
I trust life. I trust love. I trust myself.
I am open.
It is safe for me to open my heart.
I deserve love.
I am worthy to love and be loved.
It is easy for me to give and receive freely. Love is healing me now. I breathe in love with every breath I take.
My heart sings with joy and aliveness.
I am in rhythm with life.
It is safe for me to feel love.
It is safe for me to be loved.
I am forgiving. I forgive freely.
I respond in the now.
I perform my life work with ease and pleasure.
My body supports me.
I am supportive and nurturing.
Others welcome my support and power.
I let go of anger easily.
I am spontaneous and alive in my body.
I am courageous.
I am confident.
People welcome my presence.
I see myself as the worthy person I am.
It is okay for me to ask for help.
I can handle any situation.
Honesty is easy for me.
I voice my truth with clarity and integrity.
My voice is a clear channel for my heart.
It is safe to speak out.

People listen to what I have to say.
My words provide support and clarity in my relationships.
I praise God.
My words are powerful and healing.
I honor the power of the spoken word.
I carry myself with dignity and I feel it.
I am heading in the right direction.
It is easy for me to change negative thinking.
I think positive thoughts every day.
I am peaceful and calm.
I slow down my thoughts and enjoy the inner silence.
It is safe for me to know the truth.
I am intelligent.
My mind is a tool for happiness in my life.
My mind is a friend to me.
Positive thinking is easier and easier for me every day.
I release judgement.
I no longer need to judge anyone.
By letting go of judgement, I free myself and others at the same time.
I am understood.
I understand.
I look and I also see.
I am willing to look at all things in my life.
I look for the signs in life to guide me.
I see and I am seen.
I see within.
I hear and also listen.
It is safe for me to hear the truth.
When I stop thinking, and it is safe to do so, I hear the Witness.

I hear what others are saying to me.
I am open to the guidance of the Witness.
I am.
I love the Lord my God, with all my heart, with all my mind, with all my soul, and with all my strength.

ABOUT

Personal Presence And
<u>Self-Empowerment Training</u>

I have learned that a successful training process for both individuals and groups is essentially based on the true meaning of the Latin word "educare," which means "to draw from within." The premise of true education is that knowledge does not come from without. A teacher cannot teach, but can merely provide a space in which the student remembers the truth. The perceptions of truth that reside within each individual (especially when that perception is negative) are the hidden keys that unlock the potential to act from the source of true power. When the individual *owns* the knowledge, he has allowed the essence of that learning to be drawn from within his true nature.

Everyone has knowledge already available to them. They each have a Witness to their lives, past, present and future. Many people do not have access to their inner knowledge due to annoying hindrances in their subconscious that are strong enough to keep them from using the knowledge, skills and understanding already available. True educators create a space where individuals can access their knowledge from within. The purpose of my training is to connect individuals to their source of knowledge, find their inner teacher and establish conscious life-long learning. The objective is to guide the individual into experiencing his own direct perception of truth.

This book illustrates some aspects of Power of Personal Presence training. However, the experience of presence cannot really be achieved intellectually. It requires an experience and a search within for your keys in the NOW. This simply cannot be done by reading. There are major components to empowerment that involve internalizing a new definition of power that is a highly individual process. Likewise, self-judgements and core limiting perceptions which anchor all other unwanted habits of thought and behavior must be revealed. When these two dynamics are uncovered, all future endeavors of personal growth are empowered and all new learning experiences are more easily absorbed. When a participant completes this training, she often reviews her entire life in light of her new insights and revelations that are personal keys to unlock the understanding of life.

The training has proven effective for individuals in all walks of life and all ages, both men and women, couples, professionals, managers, business owners and homeworkers. Graduates are given tools to use every day for the rest of their lives—not a bag of tricks to pull out in particular situations—real and powerful tools that will never be obsolete. These are the tools for maintaining presence which will become a habit in time.

Graduates are encouraged to take these simple, practical tools and *really* use them every day. The graduates who have done so report a remarkable change in their well-being. They understand others better and are better understood. They are empowered to meet challenges in a more positive, action-oriented way. They are willing and know how to empower others in their lives. They deal better with their employees, co-workers and family members. They have higher self-esteem. They are learning to be better managers, employees, business owners, parents and individuals.

Graduates learn to express clarity, communication, confidence, caring and credibility, and enhance their image. They claim ownership of the power of their personal presence.

For information about Personal Presence and Self-Empowerment Training, please write to or call:

Image Training Center
P.O. Box 7421
16301 N.E. Eighth - Suite 230
Bellevue, Washington 98008

Phone: 206-957-1996

About The Author

Jane Hundley has spent many years working with inner and outer image analysis. She began her career as an international, editorial model working for major magazines including *Vogue, Elle,* and *Glamour* and top designers such as Oscar de la Renta, Armani, Anne Klein, Christian Dior, Valentino, Nino Cerruti, Yves St. Laurent, and many others. She has been represented by the agencies of John Casablancas and Eileen Ford. As a studio stylist, her clientele has included *The Pacific Institute, KIRO TV, Janzten, Sportswear International, New York Times, Ski Magazine, regional modeling schools, modeling agencies,* and Northwest publications. As an image consultant for Nordstrom, Jane has worked with hundreds of men and women in personal shopping, as a color and wardrobe analyst and makeup design consultant.

Jane is a currently an image consultant, registered counselor and trainer of corporate and personal development programs. She brings to her training twenty years of experience in image, self-development, meditation and movement psychology. She has designed *The Dynamics Of Personal Presence,* a training program which synchronizes body, mind, emotion and spirit through the process of self-awareness. From her dance and movement therapy background, she has developed a dynamic relaxation exercise program which helps increase strength, balance, flexibility and enhances personal presence.

Jane is a speaker and seminar leader on topics of *Personal Presence*, *Self-Empowerment,* and *Dynamic Relaxation Exercise.* She is currently living in Bellevue, Washington with her husband and two daughters, and is working toward her masters degree in applied behavioral science.

The author is available for speaking engagements.

For inquiries write or call:

Image Training Center
P.O. Box 7421
16301 N.E. Eighth - Suite 230
Bellevue, Washington 98008

Phone: 206-957-1996

To order additional copies or to send a gift of:

The Power Of
Personal Presence

Please send _____ copies at $14.95 each, plus $3 shipping and handling for the first book, $2 for each additional book.

Enclosed is my check or money order for $_____. (Please add 8.2% tax for orders sent to Washington State addresses.)

Telephone orders: Call toll free: 800-835-0220. Have your Amex, Discover, Visa or MasterCard ready.

Name_____

Company/Organization _____

Street Address _____

City/State/Zip _____

Please advise if recipient and mailing address is different from above. Surface shipping may take three to four weeks.

Please return this order form with payment to:

CenterPoint Publishing
16301 N.E. Eighth - Suite 230
Bellevue, WA 98008
Telephone: (206) 957-1996